Revamp
writings on secular Buddhism

Written with great intelligence, care and wit, *Revamp* is the most comprehensive account of secular Buddhism currently available. Ranging from the transformative inner experience of mindfulness to the social and political challenges of dharmic citizenship, Winton Higgins weaves the many diverse threads of contemporary Buddhist practice into a compelling whole. *Revamp* is an inspiring example of critical and creative thinking about the most pressing issues facing humanity in our time.
Stephen Batchelor, author of *After Buddhism*

This book is a welcome read for both secular Buddhist practitioners and those curious about it. The author elucidates the emergence, context and meeting of cultures that secular Buddhism builds on. He presents a fresh and inspiring perspective on mindfulness meditation, offering us choices of how and what to practise. Finally, he invites us to take on 'the active responsibilities of dharmic citizenship', particularly now when we face the twin crises of global warming and globalised social injustice.
Lorna Edwards, Bodhi College participant,
Secular Buddhist Network team member, Cymru Wales

Winton Higgins has played a crucial role in helping us to understand the meaning and value of a secular dharma. The essays collected in *Revamp* reveal his unmatched ability to provide us with a lucid, nuanced account of the historical roots and key philosophical ideas of secular Buddhism. At the same time, the author insightfully explores the essential practices which promote human flourishing in this world: a non-formulaic approach to insight meditation, the creation of democratic communities of practitioners, and progressive political activism to confront the two great challenges of climate change and economic injustice.
Mike Slott, editor of the Secular Buddhist Network website, New York

It is a pleasure to go on a journey with Winton Higgins from the roots of secular Buddhism as a synthesis of western philosophical influences and Asian Buddhism, to the necessary pragmatic process of change in traditional Buddhism towards a useful, liveable, and valuable Buddhism for present-day people in modern societies. Winton encourages us to get on the path to become the person we

want to be, to tackle the ills in our society, and to strengthen values that already exist. Instead of absolute truths, it is the four tasks of daily life that guide us.
Saskia Graf, meditation teacher,
Buddha-Stiftung für säkularen Buddhismus, Heidelberg

Winton Higgins's book, *Revamp*, offers a captivating and pragmatic discussion of the emergence of secular Buddhism in the west. Winton weaves together early Buddhist texts, with contemporary influences by scholars, novelists and in particular Stephen Batchelor's work, which he builds on in thoughtful and insightful ways. As an experienced teacher and practitioner, Winton addresses critical issues of understandings and of practice, tackling for example the limiting effects of celibate monasticism and gender politics. A most engaging book for readers looking to live a secular Buddhist path with authenticity and creativity.
Suzanne Franzway, secular dharma practitioner
and emeritus professor of gender studies, Adelaide, South Australia

Revamp is a short book of incredible depth and insight into secular Buddhism, one that not only tracks the movement's past along wider cultural and social currents, but also provides pointers to its exciting future. Finally, *Revamp* meets the challenge introducing people to secular Buddhism in a way that is accessible, understandable, and requires no previous knowledge of 'traditional' Buddhism.
Alex Carr, One Mindful Breath, Wellington, Aotearoa New Zealand

Though making careful connections with western and eastern philosophy and psychology, Winton Higgins continually challenges dearly held views that have underpinned much of western Buddhism. Throughout this book Winton reframes and finds new words for the four tasks as 'the kernel of the Buddha's teaching'. Each time he languages the tasks a bit differently, I become more resonant with the path I tread. If, like myself, you are not scholarly – hang in there! Reading this book takes effort, but it's well worth it. Winton's words are nectar to my heart and mind: I will read them often.
Nelly Kaufer, lead teacher, Pine Street Sangha, Portland, Oregon

Also by Winton Higgins

Love death chariot of fire (2020)

After Buddhism, a workbook (2018)

Rule of law (2016)

The magnitude of genocide with Colin Tatz (2016)

Politics against pessimism with Geoff Dow (2013)

Engine of change (2005)

Journey into darkness (2003)

Revamp
writings on secular Buddhism

Winton Higgins

Wellington
Aotearoa New Zealand

First edition April 2021

Published by
The Tuwhiri Project
PO Box 6626
Wellington 6141
Aotearoa New Zealand
www.tuwhiri.nz

Winton Higgins has waived royalty payments for this book.
All proceeds will go to The Tuwhiri Project.

ISBN 978-0-473-57139-9

A catalogue record for this book is available from the
National Library of New Zealand
Kei te pātengi raraunga o Te Puna Mātauranga o Aotearoa
te whakarārangi o tēnei pukapuka

Design John Houston
Cover by minimum graphics

Set in Fira Sans and IBM Plex Serif
Printed by IngramSpark

10 9 8 7 6 5 4 3 2 1

In memoriam Ernst Wigforss 1881–1977

Contents

Revamp: *writings on secular Buddhism*

Introduction

The term 'secular Buddhism' has appeared only in recent years, but it provides a rubric under which we can group certain spontaneous developments among some Buddhist practice groups and teachers in the west over the last four decades. Its doctrinal roots go back even further.

Most Buddhist practitioners in western countries belong to Asian diasporas and preserve the beliefs and practices of their countries of origin. The next most numerous group of practitioners consists of ethnic westerners who have adopted or adapted long-standing Asian forms of practice, with their associated rituals, beliefs and organisational culture (including discriminatory gender relations, monasticism, hierarchy, and concepts of authority). This group includes disillusioned Christians in search of an alternative religion. Neither of these groupings is secular. They tend to close ranks and hold themselves out as representing Buddhism-as-such while practising it as a religion like any other.

The third, emerging category of Buddhist practitioners in the west encompasses those who seek to develop forms of practice, community and thought that chime with their own culture and its progressive values – starting with egalitarianism, inclusiveness and democratic self-rule. Their project exemplifies what Seyla

Benhabib has called 'the flexible appropriation of tradition'.[1]

It's this third group which attracts the 'secular Buddhism' label. Prominent in its ranks are those with no prior religious affiliation or interest, including people initially drawn to Buddhism after a positive experience of mindfulness-based psychotherapy or personal training.[2] Rather than looking for an alternative religion, they're seeking a 'practical philosophy' in the ancient Greek sense – a set of ideas to practise and live by. Though religious Buddhists tend to see them as beyond the pale, secular Buddhists find their starting point in the ethics and matrix of concepts enunciated by Gotama (c. 480–400 BCE), the historical Buddha. Throughout the Buddhist world, this legacy is called 'the dharma'.

In seeking to re-articulate the dharma in their own cultural terms and for their own time, secular Buddhist practitioners are doing no more nor less than their counterparts in earlier recipient societies as the dharma spread from its ancient Indian birthplace to other Asian societies. For instance, when the Chinese gradually sinified it, starting two millennia ago, they not only made its practice accessible to themselves, but also uncovered hidden depths and possibilities in the dharma's original expression by crystallising them in terms of their own rich cultural heritage.[3] They established an excellent precedent for today's western practitioners who aspire to bring the Buddha's tradition home.

Secularity and culture

Human life as we know it depends on culture, which complements our bare neurobiological existence in much the same way as software potentiates otherwise inert computer hardware. Culture (including language) allows us to understand ourselves, our conditions of life and their inherent possibilities, and our immediate experience. And like everything else, cultures (and software) confirm an ancient Buddhist insight by arising and then being superseded according to shifting conditions.

At its core, secularity insists on the cultural specificities of time and place, and invites us to ground ourselves in them as we practise living consciously, that is, constantly returning to the root questions we all must face: 'How should I live?' and 'What sort of person should I become?' Secularity focuses on living well in this life – in this world at this time – rather than seeking salvation as beyond-human beings in some other life and world.

When Buddhists in the west follow the Chinese precedent in this secular spirit, the three great progenitors of modern western cultures open up for them – the classical heritage (including its foremost practical-philosophical schools of scepticism and epicureanism, with their striking affinities with the dharma); western Judeo-Christianity; and the culture of modernity itself, in which religious doctrine has loosened its grip on robust inquiry into our inner lives and the natural and social worlds we inhabit.

Religion and secularity

In religious thought, secularity invokes a subtle and profound trend in western religious development over the last seven centuries, one that has gained new momentum in our own time, as the philosopher Charles Taylor (a liberal Catholic) shows in his magisterial *A secular age*.[4] The medieval church promoted alternately beguiling and terrifying pictures of heaven and hell, a vengeful god, a fiendish devil, pretty angels and the gruesome deaths of martyrs. Its practice was riddled with saintly cults, and relic- and image-worship. Consistent with its ethos of religious hysteria, torture and spectacular death awaited anyone who questioned the orthodoxy. But as Taylor shows, even before the Reformation (which greatly accelerated the change) all this gradually gave way to a sober abandonment of 'superstitious uses', some of the worst aspects of dogmatism, a gradual opening to the classical heritage (and thereby humanism), and some toleration of diversity.

Fast-forward to our own time, and we find a growing number of progressive (and perhaps secular) Christian practitioners, including ordained priests and theologians (such as Don Cupitt and Lloyd Geering), who have abandoned the supernatural beliefs that today's western culture no longer supports. They seek to retrieve what Jesus actually did, said and probably meant about how to live this life well, and interpret it in terms relevant to our own times. Sofia (formerly the Sea of Faith movement in the UK, New Zealand and Australia) and the US-based Jesus Seminar, exemplify this development. They thus awaken the ire of those who continue to trade in the older certitudes. Secular dharma practitioners encounter the same push-back from conventional Buddhists.

Unsurprisingly, then, secular dharma practitioners engage in collegial public dialogue with progressive Christians, who first announced their presence in the 1950s and 1960s. They were there before us; we have much to learn from them; and they must count as a formative influence on the development of a secular dharma in the west. A clear point of convergence is that both the Buddha and Jesus, in their several idioms, taught an ethical way of life based on reflectivity, integrity, generosity, compassion and human solidarity, and used the same metaphor for it – a path. Not a belief system, not a badge of identity or of ethnic belonging, but rather a meaningful way of life or path of practice that doesn't need to be buttressed by extravagant claims about matters beyond our accessible sensory world.

So secularity has no initial argument with religion as such. Indeed, it is the product of western religious development, as Taylor argues, and the concept of 'secular religion' has gained acceptance.[5] But secularity finds little welcome at the table of institutionalised religions, such as the old Christian denominations and the often even older Buddhist monastic orders. Institutions as such tend to forget their original purposes while pursuing their more pressing interest in perpetuating themselves, and consolidating and extending their own social and political power.

Religious institutional elites have typically pursued these ends in alliances with similarly entrenched temporal elites, for whom they have provided political legitimation – not least in wartime – and social integration around elite moral codes. Brian Victoria's Zen at war illustrates this relationship well enough.[6] With a wink at the military theorist Carl von Clausewitz, one may say that institutional religion (like war) is the continuation of politics by other means. It tends to resist substantive change, and in particular to defend timeless beliefs, which are its enduring stock-in-trade. Its hostility to a harbinger of change like secularity is thus a given.

Secular Buddhism lays great emphasis on returning to the early dharmic teachings and applying them to the way we live now. Its orthodox critics often denounce this productive activity in literalist terms, which is ironic given that they themselves often hold to a version of 'the pristine dharma' that comes from the third-century BCE Abhidhamma – possibly the most drastic re-engineering of the Buddha's teaching ever.

There is a wider point here. All the myriad expressions of Buddhism, including the Buddha's own, are mediated by culture (encompassing language, and ambient beliefs and assumptions). That is why there is no pristine dharma, no Buddhist gold standard,[7] any more than we can identify a pristine Christianity. We have to accept that we are self-interpreting beings living in a shifting interpreted world, and learn to work with both. Thus there is no solid ground from which fideists can declare secular Buddhism anathema.

Buddhism and science

In the west in the late nineteenth century, Buddhism attracted the sobriquet of 'scientific religion', amid the controversy between evolutionary biology based on Charles Darwin's work, and Christian cosmology based on the book of Genesis. The concurrent emergence of the 'science' of the mind – psychology – reinforced the association. Buddhism had no creation myth or cosmology of its own to be threatened by Darwin's findings. And it had a developed interest in the mind, so it could collegially compare notes with psychologists. But that is as 'scientific' as Buddhism ever got: it could comfortably co-exist with western science, where traditional Abrahamic religions could not, and the 'science' label made for a nice selling point among the western cognoscenti.

According to a widespread perception, today's secular Buddhism owes a great deal to science, or perhaps to *scientism* understood as a sub-culture around science and its celebrity representatives, such as 'the new atheists' and some neuroscientific publicists. That perception notwithstanding, it's hard to see how secular Buddhism has gained any more substance from these sources than Buddhism as a whole has taken from natural science over the last 150 years.

Because of its post-metaphysical leanings, secular Buddhism has no interest in 'the God question'. And today's flood of new findings from neuroscience sheds little new light on the questions about how we should live, and how we should best practise the dharma as a reflective (self-interpreting) discipline. In Ludwig Wittgenstein's terms, religion and science are separate language games that pretend to ultimate 'truth' while expressing helpful insights about the human condition. But the dharma constitutes yet another language game with a vocabulary for interpreting ourselves as we work to make the most of our ethical human potential.

Secular Buddhism is not a 'school' of Buddhism: it has no orthodoxy, no separate canon, and no institutional presence bar websites. For the most part its sympathisers participate in lay practice
communities (sanghas) with dharma friends of other Buddhist
persuasions or of none in particular. Rather, secular Buddhism
stands for a developmental direction that's typically Buddhist in
its open-minded scepticism and its desire to let the dharma speak
most effectively – in culturally available terms.

Buddhism and the ethic of care

The Buddha's last days of life are recorded in some detail in the
Mahāparinibbāna sutta. Here we find him eighty years old and
terminally ill, but as lucid as ever. His very last words, spoken to
his closest followers, were: Things fall apart; tread the path with
care.[8] Given the occasion, we can appreciate how this admonition
enjoys critical importance.

We ourselves and everything in our world arise and pass
away, because the conditions supporting our existence are constantly changing, pulling the rug from under us. So things obviously manifest and then fall apart the whole time. That's basic
Buddhism, and these days basic science. The term that bears most
weight in these famous last words is the final one: *appamāda* in Pali,
the canonical language – best translated as 'care'. It's a key term
in the Buddha's working vocabulary, because care is the key to the
ethic he taught. 'Just as the footprints of all living beings that walk
fit into the footprint of an elephant, so care is the one thing that
secures all kinds of good.'

He returned to this point and analogy again and again.
'Whatever wholesome states there are, they are all rooted in care,
converge on care, and care is considered the chief among them.'[9]

Care thus underpins the four emotional settings of the awakening mind: universal friendliness, compassion, sympathetic joy, and equanimity. We can't live ethically without caring about ourselves and others, and how we interact. Moreover – as the famous last words suggest – care must suffuse our approach to practice. We can't be mindful without caring about what is happening here and now. Care underpins the radical attention that dharma practice is all about.

As both noun and verb, the English word 'care' contains many modalities depending on context and the preposition (of, for, about) that may follow it. The same is true of its Pali equivalent, appamāda. But the latter is actually in negative form and goes one better in implicitly alluding to the mind states that care must overcome. It literally means non-carelessness, non-uncaringness, non-indifference.

As we move through the sources of secular Buddhism's ethics, practice and politics in this book, we need to remember that 'they are all rooted in care', as are the western affinities that we adduce along the way.

This book

This book consists mainly of lightly edited essays I have published before, and talks I have given over the last eight years. For reasons already given, none of them lay claim to being an authoritative text for secular Buddhism. Part I presents more discursive, conceptually dense pieces that account for the rise of secular Buddhism. They locate it within western culture, and identify some of the currents of thought that mould it. Earlier versions of the first two of these chapters appeared in the *Journal of Global Buddhism*. The third chapter started as a short paper I gave at the 2013 colloquium on secular Buddhism at the Barre Center for Buddhist Studies in Massachusetts.

For the most part, the rest of the book builds on dharma talks to various practice communities in Sydney and Wellington. For this reason it's an 'easier read'. Part II makes connections with certain modern western thinkers who help us to expand on dharmic themes that are especially acute in our time and culture. Part III addresses our inner world (our interiority) – how we can occupy it and transform it. From there, part IV explores the ways in which we express our interiority in concert with others, in our ethics and culture, and in the face of a calamity like the current Covid-19 pandemic. These issues lead us into Part V, about how we humans might hope to survive and thrive on a planet plagued by existential threats, above all the twin crises that predate Covid-19 and will postdate it: the wilful despoliation of the planet and its biosphere, and the mushrooming social inequities that accompany it.

Notes

1   Benhabib 1992: 111.
2   See Batchelor 2012.
3   See for instance Safran 2003: 14–20.
4   Taylor 2007.
5   See for instance Geering 2007.
6   Victoria 2006.
7   Faure 2009.
8   I'm adopting Stephen Batchelor's (2015: 101–5) translation and interpretation of *appamāda* here.
9   *Samyutta nikāya* 45: 140: 1551.

Revamp: *writings on secular Buddhism*

Part I
Emergence

Chapter 1

The coming of secular Buddhism: a synoptic view

Naïveté is now unavailable to anyone, believer or unbeliever alike.
Charles Taylor[1]

Twenty-five years ago I started teaching Buddhist meditation (mainly what was then called *vipassanā*) in a large lay-based dharma centre cum monastic hermitage outside Sydney, one with links to the Theravādin monastic network. What I taught was formulaic, reasonably orthodox, and raised no Theravādin eyebrows. Everyone concerned belonged to the broad church of Buddhist modernism, even if tensions were already high around those aspects of the Theravāda untouched by modernity – the marginalisation of women, male monastic privilege, and an organisational culture which concentrated power at the top of a hierarchical organisation. We the disenfranchised non-hierarchs saw these failings as relics we could soon scrap, so that the Buddhism we practised would shine forth as what we naïvely assumed it to be in essence – proto-modern, rational, democratic, inclusive, and amenable to gender equality.

Ten years later the dharma centre in question imploded in the hierarchs' manful attempt to simulate an orthodox Thai Theravādin monastery in the Australian wilderness, with male monastic privilege and exclusivity once more in full bloom. The

Buddhist-modernist compromise collapsed in acrimony; goannas and wombats reclaimed the splendid acres where lay retreatants once mindfully walked.[2] Together with other teachers of similar background, I found myself teaching non-formulaic insight meditation retreats in various venues typically rented from Catholic nuns, and at weekly practice evenings in suburban insight meditation groups called *sanghas.*

These sanghas are all self-generating and have no organisational links to each other apart from membership of a lay-Buddhist peak organisation, but they march to the same drum. They're self-evidently inclusive, egalitarian and democratic – voluntary associations like any other, the stuff of civil society – free of ritual (including formulaic meditation). Their members study the original teachings of the Buddha in their historical context, in order to deepen into their dharma practice in their own intellectually free-ranging way. They trade tips on books, blogs, podcasts and websites. Ethically, their conception of dharma practice extends beyond the five precepts to tackling the big issues of today's globalised world – such as climate change and the treatment of refugees – and many are active in progressive social movements or community work. None of these sanghas identifies with the Theravāda or any other ancestral school of Buddhism.

Not long after that transition I queried an overseas visitor's use of the expression 'secular Buddhism' – what could that possibly refer to? But on reflection no alternative presents itself to capture the changes that had already occurred and were intensifying in the meditation practice and sangha life around me. Willy-nilly, secular Buddhism was upon us, ruffling fideist feathers, prompting panics and alarums, and drawing rancorous anathemas.[3]

The changes in the Sydney 'dharma scene' seem to merely exemplify shifts occurring elsewhere and in some other Buddhist schools, mostly in the English-speaking world. Though globalisation tends to diffuse cultural trends in short order, I see little evidence so far of secular Buddhist practice outside Anglophone countries, with some exceptions in the German-, Spanish- and Portuguese-speaking ones. In any event, I won't speculate here about secular Buddhism's possible diffusion elsewhere.

In this chapter, then, I embrace the expression 'secular Buddhism', together with the movement emerging in its name. I will seek to place it historically and conceptually, rather than try to pre-empt its doctrinal development. My opening *mise en scène* suffices as a preliminary marker of the secular-Buddhist condition, which answers to the need to resolve incoherences in Buddhist modernism (the 'push' factor), while responding to secularising impulses in contemporary western society (the 'pull' factor).

More generally, as my opening narrative indicates, secular Buddhism betokens a new stage in the acculturation of the dharma in the west. My account draws on Charles Taylor's œuvre, though he himself exercises an option (Christian belief) different to the one I'm presenting here. I draw on him indirectly through the influence of his *Sources of the self* on insightful accounts of Buddhist modernism, and more directly on his *A secular age* – his historical analysis of the drawn-out secular turn in the west.[4] The latter establishes a model for tracing the sources of transformations in religious-spiritual-ethical life to manifold shifts in cultural, socio-economic, political, and institutional affairs. In the background, the classical sociologist Max Weber's analysis of modernity informs Taylor's work.

My story thus starts with Buddhist modernism, out of which secular Buddhism is gradually crystallising. The former, an increasingly fraught mix of ancestral Buddhism and modern discursive practices, initially deflected European colonialism's Christianising mission in Asia and provided a bridge for missionary Buddhism's entry into the west. But internally Buddhist modernism has harboured incongruities at the levels of practice, doctrine and institutions, ones which have obstructed the dharma's deeper acculturation in the new host societies, not least as the latter have themselves been undergoing a marked cultural shift during the last half-century. Secular Buddhism constitutes one response to the impasse. In the second part of this chapter I'll go into the modalities of contemporary secularity that mould this response.

Secular Buddhism leans towards what Charles Taylor calls an 'exclusive humanism', that is, a discourse and set of practices in aid of full human flourishing – one that disavows superhuman agencies and supernatural processes, and thus redemptive ('soteriological') exits from the human condition.[5] It seeks a renewal of the Buddha's tradition, firstly by retrieving the early teachings free of later monastic commentarial spin; and secondly by developing affinities between it and fertile social practices and intellectual developments in western societies. I will focus mainly on the post-Theravādin experience, which provides something close to a paradigmatic case in the shifts involved in this story. For the most part I leave it to the reader to qualify my remarks for the legatees of other branches of ancestral Buddhism.

The modernist historical compromise

Heinz Bechert appears to have coined the term 'Buddhist modernism'.[6] But its origins go back to the latter half of the nineteenth century, especially in Sri Lanka.[7] In brutal summary, its course has run like this. Under the umbrella of British colonial rule, Christian (mainly Protestant) missionaries sought conversions among Sinhalese Buddhists, some of whose leaders resisted by adopting modern Buddhist practices along 'Protestant' lines without disturbing existing institutions or folk observance. They thus gave more weight to lay practice and study, including laicising meditation practice and making some canonical texts available to a much wider readership, not least in the rising (and increasingly educated) middle class. Soon this form of resistance to Christianised western cultural hegemony spread to Japan, Burma and Thailand, and then further afield in Buddhist Asia. As it did so, it challenged Christianity on a point on which the latter was taking a hit in its homelands: the perceived clash between Christian doctrine and ascendant scientific rationalism. Buddhism, by contrast, gained a reputation for meshing with the scientific worldview, and indeed, for being a 'scientific religion'.[8] The 'new Buddhism', as it was sometimes also called, proved amenable not only to rationalism, but also to the Romantic reaction against rationalism in the west. Thus equipped, Buddhist modernism established its own bridgeheads on western soil from the 1960s, and today it is practised on every continent in the world.

Premodern Buddhism was ever and remains a mosaic of disconnected canons, doctrines, local social practices, institutions, beliefs and folkways. In fact, the totalising concept 'Buddhism' was a European 'discovery' of the 1820s, one first proclaimed in print two decades later by the French Sanskrit scholar, Eugène Burnouf.[9] Now Buddhist modernism melded this ancestral mosaic with core but discordant themes of western modernity, and it was this modernist hybrid that came to stand for Buddhism as such from its arrival in the west.

It follows from the above synopsis that Buddhist modernism was never designed to sweep through the Buddhist world as an all-reforming, homogenising force. Nor has it. For most Asian Buddhists – both those who have stayed at home and those who have migrated to the west and joined ethnic diasporas – ancestral Buddhist life and observance persevere largely untouched by modern innovations. So at the heart of Buddhist modernism is an historical compromise – a *compromesso storico* in the Italian sense, to be compared with the coalition between Christian Democrats and Communists in postwar Italy, whereby diametrically opposed formations cooperated to achieve certain temporarily converging objectives.

David McMahan offers an insightful study of today's Buddhist modernism,[10] and I want to briefly follow his analysis to make
my point. In his second chapter, he dramatises the 'spectrum'
of current 'tradition and modernism' by building up five representative profiles of present-day Buddhist practitioners, from a
lowly Thai villager at one extreme to a highly educated female
Jewish-American dharma teacher at the other. Far from presenting
as co-religionists sharing a faith-based identity, these individuals
inhabit parallel universes, with radically diverging assumptions,
values, beliefs, practices and ways of life.

The main 'discourses of modernity' and their effects together comprise one party to the compromise in question. As we'll
see, secular Buddhism has inherited its DNA. Linda Woodhead
and Paul Heelas, and then David McMahan, follow Charles Taylor
in developing an account of them.[11] Like Taylor, they present them
not as mere ideas but as the foundations of 'the modern *identity*',
constituent elements of our forms of life.

As we've seen, Protestantism is the first of these discourses, to the extent that the earliest version of Buddhist modernism
attracted the sobriquet 'Protestant Buddhism'.[12] In its homelands
Protestantism subverted clerical intercession between God and his
creatures; it stripped religious powerholders of their charismatic
authority; it insisted on the primacy of an interiorised piety in the
individual's direct relationship with God over communal practices
and rituals. Protestantism thereby replaced external, institutionalised religious authority with the 'internal' one of the individual's
own realisation; and it frowned on 'superstitious' folk beliefs and
practices, such as festivals and image- and relic-worship. It thus
engendered individualism, interiority, and what came to be known
– after Friedrich Schiller and Max Weber – as 'the rationalisation
and disenchantment of the world'.

In this way Protestantism prepared the ground for the second of the three fundamental modern discourses – scientific rationalism, part of the heritage from the European Enlightenment. In this outlook, the world (including ourselves) is entirely bound by immanent natural laws which are discoverable and constitute complete explanations of what exists and how it develops. To anticipate Taylor's later work, this means that our lives and contexts belong to an order driven by an exclusive immanent logic: extraneous agents such as God, angels and wood sprites have no place in 'the immanent frame'.

The rationalist outlook in turn provoked the third of the discourses in question – the Romantic reaction, which John Keats, in his 1819 poem *Lamia*, pithily announced with the complaint:

> Philosophy will clip an Angel's wings,
> Conquer all mysteries by rule and line,
> Empty the haunted air.

In the upshot, Romanticism did not so much succeed in 're-enchanting' the world as in reasserting the value of emotion, passion and creativity in our lives, which makes it a progenitor of later expressive individualism and 'the psychological turn'.

As Taylor points out, together these modern discourses established two thematic emphases: a world-affirming stance that hailed the good life cultivated in this earthly existence, instead of pining for otherworldly planes of blissful existence; and a shift towards interiority and individual introspection.

The other party to the historical compromise is ancestral Buddhism in all its canonical, commentarial, institutional and folkloric diversity. The canons of all its schools are markedly 'enchanted' – the Mahāyānic ones exorbitantly so, but even the far more down-to-earth Pali canon contains not only the Buddha's own teachings but also its fair share of miracles, as well as devas and other sprites. Various takes on rebirth make for a shared enchantment across the ancestral board. In the Theravāda, the Buddha's own teachings in the Pali canon suffer severe commentarial displacement and no little disenchantment. The bulk of its doctrine and practices comes from the later *Abhidhamma*, and Buddhaghosa's fifth-century CE *Path of purification*, the idiom and substance of both of which vary markedly from the Pali canon.[13]

Monasticism casts a longer shadow over ancestral Buddhism than over any other religious tradition, and that shadow stretches farthest over the Theravāda. Here monasticism as such enjoys a metahistorical sanctity, unlike the impermanent, historically contingent institutions encountered throughout recorded history. Monks constitute both a priestly class and a gender-exclusive spiritual elite to the extent that the laity suffer a Feuerbachian alienation. The monks ply the full gamut of spiritual practice – only they enjoy the boon of *sangha* (spiritual community), and all religious authority resides in their hierarchs; while the laity's practice consists largely in supporting the monks and their practice. Two articles of faith ensue: only monks can achieve enlightenment, and only practices sanctioned by them enjoy validity.

Here we've come a long way from the animating discourses of modernity, even before we arrive at the single most destabilising factor in the modernity-exposed Theravāda today – the exclusion of women from full ordination. In the postwar world, where the ethical commitment to our common humanity is globally enshrined in such UN compacts as the 1948 Universal declaration of human rights and the 1979 Convention on the elimination of all forms of discrimination against women, the exclusion of women fundamentally transgresses what Taylor calls 'the modern moral order'.[14]

The travails of the modernist compromise

As Buddhism was making landfall in the west from the 1960s, neophyte Buddhists lacked the familiarity to discern and challenge the incongruities and regressions that lurked beneath the seamless, modernity-friendly façade of Buddhism as the historical compromise rendered it. In time, though, the naivety lifted and the now visible incongruities unleashed a number of destabilising processes that McMahan identifies as *demythologisation, detraditionalisation*, and the reaction against the latter – *retraditionalisation*.[15] (It was the latter that destroyed the dharma centre I referred to at the beginning of this chapter).

To these processes we must add the controversial and complex process of *psychologisation*. For nigh on a century commentators have acknowledged common ground between some of the myriad forms of both Buddhist and western psychological practice. That they can creatively cross-fertilise, as Jeremy Safran and his collaborators exemplify, is hardly controversial.[16] Controversy does arise, however, when Buddhism is reduced to a psychology or psychotherapy like any other, and when particular Buddhist practices are isolated, decontextualised, commodified and then marketed as standalone therapies trading on the Buddhism brand.[17] The psychotherapeutic model also infects Buddhist meditators. Some self-pathologise and look to Buddhist practices for 'cures'. So they lace their practice with 'curative fantasies'.[18]

We can all rejoice when psychotherapists repurpose certain Buddhist practices to good therapeutic effect, but the redeployment itself normally occurs on an individualistic, fee-for-service basis at a considerable remove from Buddhism's dharmic, communal and ethical framework, including the principle of making the dharma freely available. The Buddhist branding is thus deceptive. The problem intensifies in the face of such contemporary phenomena as 'the happiness industry' and 'the modern mindfulness movement' with their apotheoses in expensive corporate events bearing such names as 'Happiness and its Causes' and 'Mind and its Potential', and panels combining berobed Buddhist dignitaries (such as the Dalai Lama) with jet-setting neuroscientists. The Buddhism brand then becomes a fashion label.

Two related areas of naïveté within Buddhist modernism remain, however, even in the works of our principal guides above, and they vitally concern secular Buddhism. The first attaches to the promiscuous use of the word 'tradition' to denote the imagined unity and sacred authority of whatever we've inherited, that which (in the narratives of its would-be defenders)[19] now supposedly finds itself desecrated by secular-Buddhist writers. This usage equates tradition with some ill-defined *ancien régime*, the significance of which term I'll return to below.

Alasdair MacIntyre provides us with a more useful notion of tradition as an *intergenerational conversation* that informs and holds any practice worthy of the name – a conversation whose participants know what the founder's generative questions were. 'A tradition may cease to progress or may degenerate,' he writes. '[W]hen a tradition is in good order it is always partially constituted by an argument about the goods the pursuit of which give to that tradition its particular point or purpose...Traditions, when vital, embody continuities of conflict.'

In this way MacIntyre characterises a *living* tradition as one which reveals 'those future possibilities which the past has made available to the present'. A *dead* (or 'sedimented') tradition, by contrast, is one in which the generative questions have been lost, along with knowledge of how the conversation has developed since the founder(s) first articulated them. The practitioners of a dead tradition are thereby condemned to merely defend, preserve and re-enact the certitudes and rituals into which they've been inducted.[20]

Seen through this prism, secular Buddhists – with their penchant for examining afresh the earliest texts, asking probing questions and adapting the teachings to the time and culture in which we live – stand out as upholders of the Buddha's living tradition rather than as apostates. In which case, what are we to make of the claims of their 'traditionalist' critics?

This question requires us to tackle the second surviving naïveté inherent in Buddhist modernism, one concerning the status of monastic doctrine and practice, which seem to go to the core of the traditionalists' sense of what constitutes 'the tradition'. Monastic life is 'traditionally' not seen as a mere personal choice, comparable to alternative choices of ways of life, but rather as an incomparably superior one commanding deference. By comparison, lay life and practice can only ever amount to a pale imitation. Only monks attract the title 'venerable'; their way of life and practice constitutes the template against which all others are evaluated.

In particular, the naivety here consists in assuming that the monastic institutions in question have functioned as merely neutral, high-minded incubators of doctrine and practices whose genetic makeup was already established at the dawn of the tradition. It's as if the nature of the incubators themselves has exercised no formative influence at all on their products. This implicit assumption of institutional neutrality is not unique to Buddhism – it underpins most narratives of religious institutional and doctrinal development in which references to institutional power, interests and dynamics are suppressed. Yet – to return to the Buddhist case – power suffuses monasticism at every turn. All substantial organisations, not least hierarchical ones such as monasteries, generate power relations and internal power struggles. The external power relations that monastic orders participate in include alliances with temporal authorities, bolstering monastic authority over lay people, and men's authority over women. In many Buddhist countries, such as Thailand and Sri Lanka, monasticism plays an important role, typical of religious institutions in general, of social integration around established mores and legitimation of established temporal elites, who in turn patronise the monastic hierarchs.[21]

Monasteries are thus power-full institutions on several levels, and they require a disciplined cadre to retain their cohesion and reproduce patterns of domination and subordination. What appears on the surface as a rigorous spiritual training for spiritual seekers also exemplifies the sort of discursive disciplinary power that Michel Foucault analysed – the drilling of minds and bodies in the service of a regimented personal development focused on 'purity'.[22]

As noted earlier, the operative discourse arises from the *Abhidhamma* and Buddhaghosa's *The path of purification.* They are both monastic commentaries, despite the official retrofitting of the Abhidhamma into the Pali canon as the 'third basket' after the Buddha's actual teachings – the discourses (*suttas*) and the monastic rule (*vinaya*). Buddhist modernism's laicised, formulaic *vipassanā* meditation practices have their roots in this discursive practice, and impose the template for renunciant monastic life and practice on retreats, even on those practitioners leading markedly divergent lay lives.

In the mid-twentieth century an ancestor of secular Buddhism, Ñaṇavīra Thera, pointed out how the Pali commentaries in question bent the Buddha's dharma out of shape. Having identified those texts that do contain the Buddha's own teachings, he comments: 'no other Pali books whatsoever should be taken as authoritative; and ignorance of them (and particularly of the traditional Commentaries) may be counted a positive advantage, as leaving less to be unlearned.'[23]

He wouldn't have been surprised to observe how the monastic template of spiritual practice on and off the cushion has proved markedly inappropriate for many westerners, an experience that has renewed the call to 'unlearn' it, not least in its technical and formulaic approaches to insight meditation.[24] Though 'Buddhist meditation' as a job lot is sold as a royal road to modernist interiority and introspection, in formulaic guise it actually deflects and short-circuits the inward probe, as so much of our actual meditative experience falls outside the template, to be rejected as 'not meditation'.

That formulaic 'Buddhist meditation' has found a home in some western psychotherapies, not least cognitive behavioural therapy (CBT), may then seem ironic. But as Darian Leader points out, CBT too leaves the intricacies of the patients' lives and experience – their subjectivity – unexamined, and 'is a form of conditioning that aims at mental hygiene'.[25] There is a striking elective affinity between normalising Abhidhamma-based meditative techniques and a notion of mental hygiene that merely suppresses symptoms. Both fail as vehicles of modern interiority.

The secular trajectory

Secular Buddhism constitutes one attempt to overcome the incongruities of the Buddhist modernist compromise. It seeks to renew the Buddha's tradition by abandoning the anomalous vestiges of ancestral Buddhism – including monastic organisational and meditative culture reworked in laicised form – as a prelude to bringing the dharma into a deeper connection with today's western sensibilities and way of life. (Its arrival, however, hardly heralds the end of Buddhist modernism, on whose protean nature too many vested interests and careers continue to depend.) Why, and in what sense, this response is 'secular' is by no means obvious, and I will now attempt to sketch some of its sources and possible lines of development.

As a preliminary observation we should note the poignant

etymology of 'secular' in the Latin *saeculum* – originally a human life span, later specified as a century, as in the French *siècle*. As already hinted, contributors to secular Buddhism return to the Buddha's own teachings while cultivating a sense of their historical context as a hermeneutic strategy.[26] This practice aligns with today's contextualist (or 'Cambridge') school of historical interpretation that reads significant historical texts as initiatives taken in (and witnessing to) concrete historical predicaments in which the authors were embedded, rather than as contextless iterations of timeless truths.[27] In this approach, the Buddha appears not as a religious messiah but more like a contemporary Greek philosopher addressing human predicaments in turbulent times, and attracting a following which forms communities committed to living by his teaching.[28]

The attention to *saecula* applies equally to how we in our own time and context receive and deploy these intimations from the past. Instead of lapsing into a fundamentalism around what the Buddha arguably 'really' meant, we take advantage of what Gianni Vattimo calls 'the productiveness of interpretation' (or 'ontological hermeneutics').[29] This approach can add something essential to texts so that they can better address our own contexts and predicaments.

That said, in common parlance (helped along by today's best-selling militant atheists) 'secularity' evokes a challenge to religion, and signifies religion's retreat from social and individual lives, supposedly as science advances an alternative and more convincing worldview. According to mainstream secularisation theory, the European Enlightenment and scientific rationalism trumped the enchanted religious imaginary with its attendant pieties and sensibilities. One of Charles Taylor's many achievements consists in overthrowing this naïve thesis, in the first instance in 'the North Atlantic world' on which he focuses. He dubs the variations on the thesis 'subtraction theories' which imply that as science debunks religious myths and subtracts them from our reality constructs, secular truth replaces them. Helpfully, he disaggregates secularity into three related aspects: the falling away of the religious under- and overlays of our public institutions; the decline in popular religious belief and observance; and the changed '*conditions of belief*' – or 'contexts of understanding' – whereby we have moved over several centuries from a condition of virtually unchallengeable belief in God to one wherein belief 'is understood to be one option among others, and frequently not the easiest to embrace'.[30]

In setting up his inquiry in this way, Taylor makes a vital philosophical move out of the barren, view-from-nowhere epistemological stance that invites questions such as 'Does God exist?' or 'Do we really get reborn?' This is the stance from which most polemics against secular Buddhism (and Christian belief, for that matter) are conducted in the form of endless clashes without winners between proponents of ancient and modern truth-claims respectively. Instead, he follows Heidegger in particular in framing questions of belief in terms of the engaged agent's 'pre-ontological' cultural background and situated experience.[31] Our embeddedness in a particular culture and its stage of development (our 'conditions of belief', among other things) moulds our receptivity or resistance to various values and beliefs.

The first two aspects of secularity listed above are essentially matters of record. It is by inquiring into the dynamic process driving the third aspect – the real subject of Taylor's monumental work – that we can also come to grips with the way in which Anglophone societies have received and adapted Buddhism since the 1960s. In his historical analysis of the Christian experience, Taylor introduces a number of ideal types based on periodisations that help us to periodise the Buddhist-modernist development, even if the historical breaks in the Buddhist world lag those of the Christian one.

Especially before the Reform period (roughly 1450–1650), western Christendom clove to the *ancien régime* (AR) ideal type: one was baptised into and learned to participate in 'the Church' as a matter of course; it and its truth-claims had no rivals – in this sense belief was 'naive'; its structures were based on the sacred/profane binary, its enchanted stories, beliefs, rituals and festivals had been there since 'time out of mind' and constituted the very fabric of one's reality and way of life. Religion was something communally enacted in order to win favour with benevolent supernatural forces and ward off the malevolent ones.

But the Reform period gradually destabilised the AR-type church. Reformers frowned on 'superstition', and the 'carnality' of festivals; they encouraged the laity to pursue a more disciplined, 'pious' way of life, and to practise self-examination as a form of piety – a first move towards later interiority and individuation. And they rebelled against the elevation of a renunciant priesthood over the laity.[32] Rival versions of religious reform clashed in often large-scale, bloody conflicts, with half-reformed Catholicism pitted against various versions of Protestantism. Some states (revolutionary America and France in particular) distanced themselves from these conflicts and from any institution claiming to represent an established national church.

In time, this 'disestablishmentarianism' would enshrine the separation of church and state in virtually all western countries. Thus the conditions of belief were already changing drastically away from birth into a self-evident 'one true faith' before the rise of scientific rationalism. Much of what we recognise today as hallmarks of secularity in fact emerged from endogenous religious developments which in turn impacted on western culture, including the European Enlightenment. They had little to do with a supposed victory march of 'science'.

Today progressive versions of Christianity can give an

enhanced account of their tradition without the baggage of the Genesis creation myth, the virgin birth, the physical resurrection, and even God as an external entity.[33] Max Weber's classic study of Protestantism and the rise of capitalism also points to the religious sources of secularity.[34] Following Nietzsche and Heidegger, Gianni Vattimo comes to the same conclusion: 'The death of God, of the moral-metaphysical God, is an effect of religiosity.' He, too, mounts a powerful case for Christianity's role as 'source and condition for the possibility of secularity'.[35] We may note a similar pattern in the Buddhist case: the authors of the earliest secular-Buddhist texts (Ñaṇavīra Thera and Stephen Batchelor) were both monks at the time.[36]

In Taylor's account we then come to 'the age of mobilisation', roughly 1800–1960, which fostered the M (for 'mobilisation') type of religious institution, typically represented by an ever growing number of 'denominations'. The latter had clearly not existed since time immemorial. An individual committed to one of them as a matter of personal choice and conscience; they and their assets had to be built up, often from humble beginnings. The faithful lived largely in a modern, disciplined, disenchanted, soul-searching world. Their piety expressed itself in their orderly work, family and church lives, and their attention to civic duty. Being a Christian meant being a robust citizen of one's community and nation. Here we find the origins of America's 'civil religion'.[37] Religious choice and piety were individual responsibilities, further aspects of individuation, even when they fostered a communitarian ethic.

The drastic cultural turn of the 1960s broke that nexus between individualism and communitarian mobilisation, in Taylor's analysis. The turn took individuation even further and sacralised individual authenticity – hence his dubbing the current stage 'the age of authenticity' – at the expense of communal integration.[38]

Authenticity emerged as a significant theme in early and

mid-twentieth century philosophy (Heidegger, Sartre, Camus), and became a central trope in a new twist on western culture driven by expressive individualism. The demands for solidarity and conformity of the M-type denominations fell foul of spiritual seekers' demand for teachings and practices that could unreservedly contain their own personalised inward quests, which themselves had good Christian antecedents going back through Protestantism to medieval German mystics such as Meister Eckhart.

The pluralistic pattern of religious life in the age of mobilisation now exploded (in Taylor's metaphor) in a 'nova effect'. The spiritual seeker faces unlimited options, and under these drastically changed conditions of belief, no particular option could credibly hold itself out as the one true faith or way, or the 'true' reading of the sacred texts in question. Nor could the non-deluded chooser imagine that s/he had encountered and espoused the one true faith rather than simply exercised a personal choice. This logic applies with equal force to Buddhism which, as Bernard Faure argues, never has presented one true form or essential doctrine in the first place.[39] Those who inveigh against secular Buddhism in the name of 'traditional' or 'true' Buddhism, or 'what the Buddha really meant', rehearse the very naivety that Taylor declares no longer available.

From the western perspective, the coming of Buddhism in its manifold and proliferating forms in the latter twentieth century simply contributed to the nova effect. To shift metaphors, the spiritual smorgasbord just expanded a little further. Taylor's ideal types help clarify the dynamic within Buddhist circles in the west. Here Buddhist modernism has manifested both in monastic forms that align with Taylor's AR type (maintained by diasporic communities and western retraditionalisers in the main), and other, modernising laicised forms reminiscent of the denominations of his M type. Some of the latter, such as Gaia House in England, and

Spirit Rock and the Insight Meditation Society in the USA, have mobilised robustly around reformed teaching and practices, and thus gained prominence.

But Buddhists lack the Christian taste for spirited contention, and baulk at 'embodying continuities of conflict' as MacIntyre would have a vital tradition do. The Buddhist ARs and Ms have co-mingled uneasily in the west in their popular front, carefully avoiding two intertwined issues that a Buddhist movement born to the age of authenticity (secular Buddhism, for instance) has no choice but to pose. The first of these issues concerns the status of the monastic template in Buddhist practice and organisational culture. The second issue involves the incompatibility between the renunciatory conception of the good life on the one hand; and on the other, the native western 'eudaimonic' conception of developing our manifold human capacities ('full human flourishing' in Taylor's phrase) on the other.

Behind these two issues lurks a third, one that preoccupies Taylor since it goes to the nub of what a 'secular age' actually is – 'one in which the eclipse of all goals beyond human flourishing becomes conceivable; or better, it falls within the range of an imaginable life for masses of people.'[40]

Or, to pose a less theistic question: can full human flourishing be pursued within the human condition – entirely within 'the immanent frame' – or must it ultimately seek to transcend it? Crudely put, does the Buddha's teaching point to a (steep) stairway to heaven, or to full human flourishing here on terra firma? Buddhist canons make both options available in manifold variations. Such are our conditions of belief today.

These three issues arrange themselves in increasing order of difficulty.

Exercising secular options

Monastic ordination in the Theravāda remains a legitimate option for a male Buddhist to choose. In the west, though, only a tiny minority do so. The rest of us dharma practitioners must take responsibility for our stance towards the male monastic norm that infuses our inherited conceptions of practice. Will we honour, as best we can, its renunciatory values and its standardising conceptions of spiritual practice, process and attainment? Or will we fashion a dharma practice that excises the monastic norm – a practice informed instead by our own cultural heritage from Greek eudaimonic thought, modern humanism and moral code, and the contemporary insistence on authenticity and individuation?[41]

The latter combination would seem to be the only one that integrates our spiritual aspirations with our embeddedness in contemporary western culture and the modern moral order. For most of us, this option alone accommodates our actual commitment to such elements of full human flourishing as free-ranging interiority, sexual love, family life, occupational fulfilment, aesthetic appreciation and self-expression, and civic and social engagement.

These two renderings of a dharmic commitment – the renunciatory and the eudaimonic – may share common elements. But as options to live by, they diverge markedly and call on us to choose between them if our spiritual lives are not to fall into incoherence. Moreover, as embedded agents in the Anglophone countries in particular, we inherit a culture in which religious reform has long since marginalised the practice and values of monasticism, not least its trope of 'purity'. We are more likely to accept Mary Douglas's anthropological assessment: the lived pursuit of purity works by rejection, and must end up in something 'poor and barren'.[42]

All options run moral risks, however, and we need to remain alert to those stalking the secular one. The age of authenticity has a narcissistic shadow side, as Christopher Lasch pointed out early in the piece; some commentators now see culturally induced narcissism reaching 'epidemic' proportions.[43] New Age spiritualities and shallower psychotherapeutic currents draw on vulgarised Buddhism; they can in turn deflect the pursuit of authenticity in its name into a narcissistic corruption that combines self-preening solipsism with ethical and civic indifference. Secular Buddhism thus has added cause to uphold its dharmic bearings and commitment to an ethic of care, as well as its membership of the modern moral order.

The third issue mentioned above that we need to tackle invokes the old transcendence-versus-immanence conundrum. For the Theravāda (as opposed to Zen, for example), the goal is to transcend (leave behind) the human condition as it is specified in the classical elements of *dukkha*: birth, sickness, old age, death, frustration and vulnerability, and thus attain an irreversible awakened *status*, angel-like arahantship 'beyond suffering'. This project normally takes several lifetimes and hence assumes rebirth. Once again, we face a stark choice between this scenario on the one hand, and on the other spiritual fulfilment (including awakening understood as *process*) within the human condition.

Martha Nussbaum mounts a powerful argument against the aspiration to transcend the human condition in a perfection and immortality alien to us – what she calls 'external transcendence'. We find this negation forcefully played out, she writes, as early as Homer's *Odyssey*, when Odysseus rejects the goddess Calypso's offer of eternal youth, beauty, life and love on her peaceful island, in order to return across the perilous 'wine-dark ocean' to his ageing-prone and mortal Penelope. If he stayed with Calypso, he would betray what he essentially is – a needy but resourceful mortal.[44]

On the other hand, Nussbaum holds out the prospect of an 'internal' transcendence, in terms I will quote *in extenso*, as they express what a secular-Buddhist aspiration might look like, not least on the back of non-formulaic insight meditation:

> There is a great deal of room for transcendence of our ordinary humanity – transcendence, we might say, of an *internal* and human sort. It is for this reason, among others, that I have taken such a deep interest in the writings of Henry James and Marcel Proust, and in their explicit claim that the artist's fine-tuned attention and responsiveness to human life is paradigmatic of a kind of precision of feeling and thought that a human being can cultivate, though most do not. Neither has the slightest interest in religious or otherworldly or even contemplative transcendence; both aim at transcendence nonetheless, and exemplify it in their writing. For I believe it is no accident at all that both James and Proust, apparently independently, compare excellent literary works to angels that soar above the dullness and obtuseness of the everyday, offering their readers a glimpse of a more compassionate, subtler, more responsive, more richly human world. That is a view about transcendence. And I believe it is extremely important to make the aspiration to that sort of transcendence central to a picture of the complete human good. There is so much to do in this area of *human* transcending (which I imagine also as a transcending by *descent*, delving more deeply into oneself and one's humanity, and becoming deeper and more spacious as a result) that if one pursued that aim well and fully I suspect that there would be little time left to look about for any other sort. And I confess that I much prefer Jamesian angels of fine-tuned perception and bewildered human grace to the angels of the religious tradition – who, as Aquinas most perceptively saw, would not be able to get

around in our world at all, since they lack imagination and the ability to perceive particulars.

On the other side, what my argument urges us to reject as incoherent is the aspiration to leave behind altogether the constitutive conditions of our humanity, and to seek for a life that is really the life of another sort of being – as if it were a higher and better life for us.[45]

The Greek warning against *hubris* reinforces the last point, she adds. Hubris comes down to 'the failure to comprehend what sort of life one has actually got, the failure to live within its limits (which are also possibilities), the failure, being mortal, to think mortal thoughts. Correctly understood, the injunction to avoid *hubris* is...an instruction as to where the valuable things *for us* are to be found.'[46]

She thus evokes the theme of our *finitude*, which potentially constitutes the central strength of secular Buddhism, and its bulwark against narcissistic grandiosity. Greek thought, myth and tragic vision locate the dignity of the mature human spirit in confronting finitude – exercising agency in the face of all its aspects as they unpredictably and implacably impact upon a human life. To live otherwise is to inhabit the world of the child, the narcissist, the childish and capricious immortal gods. Instead of fleeing finitude, we allow it to season and lend urgency to our human subjectivity. We'll go further into this topic when we meet Martin Hägglund in Part II.

Needless to say, this view of the human condition resonates with the Buddha's concept of impermanence and change (*anicca* in Pali). As we'll also see in Part II, Martin Heidegger strongly reclaims the theme in his concept of 'being-towards-death', as part of his larger theory of embodied and embedded human agency under the rubric *Dasein* ('being-there'). Vattimo extols this being-towards-death as 'a key to authentic existence.' Pascal Mercier dramatises finitude in the same vein in his novel, *Night train to Lisbon*.[47] A secular Buddhism that embraces finitude (Nussbaum's 'constitutive conditions of our humanity') still aspires to radical human transformation, as well as awakening and other epiphanies on the way, but it eschews a terminus in a timeless superhuman stasis as so much hubris.

Conclusion

I have tried to account for the coming of secular Buddhism – why it's emerging now, and what general perspectives it offers western dharma practitioners (in the first instance) in the current 'age of authenticity'. It has a longer history in the form of piecemeal, unlabelled innovations in spiritual practice, engagement with the wider culture and in its associational forms. Only now has it begun to profile itself in labelled doctrinal terms. On the one hand, it seeks to resolve incongruities in the wider Buddhist modernism, ones that foster growing spiritual incoherence. On the other hand, it answers to the call of today's secularity – a complex and frequently misunderstood religio-cultural development in the west.

Secular Buddhism's specific reason for being is to participate in that development in aid of the dharma practice of those embedded in it, while situating itself in the Buddha's living (as opposed to sedimented) tradition of practice and thought. It attracts controversy for departing from two aspects of ancestral Buddhism which often pose as Buddhism-as-such: 'enchanted' truth claims, including rebirth and a conception of superhuman transcendence; and monasticism – particularly monasticism's claim to metahistorical authority, and the renunciatory monastic norm for practice inscribed even in the laicised forms of Buddhist modernism.

Secular Buddhism can only fulfil its remit by remaining highly receptive to ancient and modern intellectual and artistic developments in the west. I have touched on a number of these, including ancient Greek thought and modern psychoanalytic theory. But the association that arises with greatest persistence is with phenomenology, and its key figure, Martin Heidegger, in particular. This association goes back a long way. In the early 1960s Ñaṇavīra Thera was already citing chapter and verse from Heidegger's *Being and time*, in his own writings. Heidegger's opus also provides the conceptual backbone of Stephen Batchelor's earliest book, *Alone with others*, which exemplifies how phenomenology provides a conceptually rich meeting point for ancient and modern thought and practice, far from the noisy arenas wherein gladiatorial truth-claims do endless battle.[48] I'll return to Heidegger's contribution in chapter 4.

While secular Buddhism's relationship with phenomenology is far from exclusive, it continues to be a peculiarly fertile one. *Being* (including becoming, engaged agency and subjectivity informed by finitude) and *time* (the time-boundedness of human life, time as the measure of change) constitute the axes around which our lives and spiritual practice unfold. Above all, phenomenology returns us to a strong sense of our embodiment previously lost to religious systems (Christian and Buddhist) that have 'excarnated' us, in Taylor's apt term. Heidegger's work, and that of Maurice Merleau-Ponty,[49] complement the Buddha's own teachings on meditation practice, ones like the *Satipaṭṭhāna sutta* which emphasise the immediacy of embodied conscious experience in the awakening process.

Chapter 2
The flexible appropriation of tradition

Stephen Batchelor has contributed most to the development of secular Buddhism this century. His contribution takes the form of many books and other published writings, as well as talks given and retreats led on five continents – the latter co-taught with Martine Batchelor. In this chapter I'll review his three books published between 2010 and 2017: *Confession of a Buddhist atheist* (2010), *After Buddhism: rethinking the dharma for a secular age* (2015), and *Secular Buddhism: imagining the dharma in an uncertain world* (2017). Together these books set out a coherent account of – and vision for – secular Buddhism in considerable depth.

In 1972 Batchelor left his native Britain and made his way to Dharamsala in India, the centre of Tibetan Buddhism in exile. There he studied in the Gelugpa tradition, ordained aged twenty-one, and underwent a rigorous monastic training for the next ten years. The latter part of his time in Tibetan robes found him working in Switzerland, then Germany. He first came to international attention as a Tibetan-English translator, starting with the publication in 1979 of his rendering of Shantideva's *Guide to the bodhisattva's way of life*. Translations of Nāgārjuna and contemporary Tibetan teachings followed.

Dissatisfied with what he saw as the scholasticism and doctrinal certitudes of Tibetan Buddhism, Batchelor moved in 1981 to Ssonggwangsa, a Korean Sŏn monastery, under the tutelage of Kusan Sunim. In 1985 he disrobed, married Martine Fages (now Martine Batchelor, a dharma teacher and author in her own right, as well as his collaborator), and entered on his present career as an independent, international dharma teacher, scholar and writer. A long list of publications lend distinction to this career, which also includes co-founding the Sharpham College for Buddhist Studies and Contemporary Enquiry and the more recent Bodhi College, and substantial input in the development of Buddhist institutions in the west (not least the insight meditation retreat centre Gaia House in the UK).

As Batchelor has worked mainly in the west, the overarching theme of adapting the dharma to western culture has steadily grown in intensity in that work. Over its two and a half millennia, the Buddhadharma has crossed many cultural boundaries, so historical precedents abound. The Chinese one, starting around two millennia ago, stands out. In China the dharma encountered an advanced civilisation whose language and culture expressed emphases, folkways, and reality constructs quite different to those of its birthplace, fifth century BCE India. After generations of acculturation, a particularly Chinese iteration of dharma and its practice, Ch'an, emerged in the seventh century CE. It was unmistakably dharma, but at the same time strikingly different from the original model.

Would the western experience of re-rooting the dharma manifest a similar contrast – only more so? Batchelor's answer to this question was a tentative yes that has become less tentative over the last three decades and in the three books under review here.

Just as the Chinese adaptation of the dharma produced Ch'an (which in turn spawned Sŏn in Korea and Zen in Japan), so secular Buddhism is one thinkable contender for the western acculturation, and the one with which Batchelor is now publicly associated. Secular Buddhism as it exists today is a developmental tendency only; it makes no claim to being an institutionalised and fully articulated 'school' of Buddhism, nor does Batchelor claim to speak authoritatively on its behalf. But we may have to wait some time for a plausible competing account to emerge and challenge the one presented in the three books I look at below.

An enduring theme in Batchelor's recent work is narrativity. We tend to make sense of things by telling stories about them, thus grasping their origins in a temporal dimension – whether through more or less mythologised histories, or through pure myths of origins. Epics such as *Gilgamesh*, the *Odyssey*, the *Iliad*, the Hebrew Bible, and the *Mahābhārata* have laid foundations for civilisations and religious traditions. Yet – apart from a mythical rendering of the Buddha's life, starting with the crown prince in the palace – the dharma has singularly eschewed the narrative of its own origins. The early texts contain no sense of historical time. The Buddha's life story and its context are fragmented and chronologically scrambled throughout the five collections (*nikāyas*) of the discourses, and the monastic rule (*vinaya*), attributed to him in the Pali canon.

An earlier British-born convert, Ñāṇamoli Bhikkhu (1905–1960), made the first attempt to unscramble the elements of the Buddha's life story and the development of his teaching.[50] Now Batchelor follows suit. His books contain layers of narrative: of the Buddha's life, of the lives of some of his associates, and of the turbulent political and socio-economic context in which these lives unfolded. He acknowledges the contributions made by GP Malalasekera and Trevor Ling to his own retrieval.[51] In this way Batchelor gleans many interpretive insights that I will return to below. For good measure, he throws in the narrative of his own spiritual trajectory, a story which accounts for the elements of Asian and western thought that have contributed to his account of the dharma.

Confession of a Buddhist atheist

Batchelor's own narrative in fact generates the structure of *Confession*, published in 2010. The book is formally divided into two parts, dealing with the author's monastic and later lay periods respectively. But the chronological arrangement of the book's eighteen chapters tracks a smooth narrative arc and cumulative development that belies this two-part division. Batchelor takes us through his many sequential sources of inspiration, uncomfortable changes in perspective, and consequent agonised leave-takings from his traditional teachers and institutions.

He honours the enduring inputs that his Tibetan and Korean teachers have made to his dharmic formation.[52] Alongside them he introduces his readers to the currents of western thought that have influenced him to the present day, ones that he sees as resonating with the dharma. These currents start in ancient Greece with the sceptics, stoics, and epicureans, and then mainly fast-forward to post-metaphysical thought since Nietzsche – phenomenology (notably Heidegger's 1927 *Being and time*), existentialism, and the philosophical pragmatism of John Dewey, William James and Richard Rorty. The modern current also includes post-metaphysical Christian theologians, from Paul Tillich and Dietrich Bonhoeffer to Batchelor's friend, Don Cupitt. Another formative influence (and yet another earlier British convert), Ñāṇavīra Thera (1920–1965), himself straddles the Pali canon and modern post-metaphysical thought. He also provides an alluring role model for a European outrider in Asia, one who digs deeply into the early dharma to radically challenge its orthodox interpretation.[53]

Enfolded in Batchelor's autobiographical narrative in *Confession* is the second draft (after Ñāṇamoli's, but in a starkly contrasting idiom) of Gotama the historical Buddha's life story. Batchelor's draft draws on the Pali canon; his own thought-provoking 2003 tour of prominent sites where Gotama grew up, awakened, lived, taught, and died; and plausible surmises and inferences about his life where the canon remains sketchy, contradictory, or altogether silent. The silence is especially loud around Gotama's formative years up to his 'going forth' into wandering mendicancy at the age of twenty-nine. Given his high-caste status, lifelong associates, and erudition, for instance, might he not – like his cohort – have received an advanced education in Tackkasila (Taxila), the intellectual centre and capital of Gandhara to the west of his native Sakiya?

In any event, the Gotama we meet here, embedded as he is in a fraught time and place, bears little resemblance to the timeless and decontextualised Buddha of conventional Buddhism. The former had to manoeuvre around and compromise with powerful but capricious rulers in order to survive and protect his following. This situated Gotama spoke from and to real-world experience, and (Batchelor argues) ought now to be heard and interpreted as having done so. 'Gotama's voice is confident, ironic, at times playful, anti-metaphysical, and pragmatic' (p. 124). Both the individual and his message thus become more intelligible and compelling for modern westerners.

In chronological order in his own narrative, Batchelor introduces virtually all the concepts and arguments that will, in the two later books, provide him with the building blocks for his edifice, secular Buddhism. Since I will consider that edifice as a whole later in this chapter, at this stage I will only briefly introduce them as they appear in *Confession*.

In his 1997 *Buddhism without beliefs*, Batchelor had already taken a sceptical stance towards the doctrine of rebirth, a stance that becomes outright rejection in *Confession*. In the Buddha's time and place, the rebirth premise underpinned the ambient religious culture, and the early dharma preserved it – de rigueur if it was to have any currency in its birthplace – while forcefully suggesting that the present life (and dharma practice in it) could never be reduced to mere preparation for the next. But in the west, Batchelor argues, rebirth doctrine actually depreciates the dharma's currency: it sits ill with western religious culture, and even worse with the secular-scientific culture of late modernity. Moreover, unwavering consciousness of human finitude and the finality of death constitute a precondition to living authentically for phenomenology and existentialism, which otherwise exhibit a strong elective affinity with the dharma (pp. 53, 156).[54]

In most societies in which Buddhism has manifested as a mass religion, belief in rebirth has played an essential role. All mass religions have served vital socio-political purposes: upholding communal cohesion and norms, and legitimating existing temporal power structures. For this reason, in virtually all religions, visions of contrasting post-mortem destinies promise redemption through transcendence to a higher plane of existence for the compliant, and threaten transgressors with damnation. 'Soteriology' is the technical term for the promise of salvation or redemption that religions offer in this way. Institutionalisation of a mass religion calls for revealed truths that support these soteriological visions, as well as institution-sustaining forms of mass observance driven by the relevant carrots and sticks of future redemption/transcendence on the one hand, and damnation on the other.

For Batchelor (as for Ñāṇavīra before him), the underlying problem lies in the dharma's reissue as a religion, which in Batchelor's account (229–235) began when Kassapa seized control of the dharmic community at the First Council shortly after Gotama's death around 400 BCE. After that, tamperings with the canon and the emergence of the whole Pali commentarial tradition served the purpose of adapting the dharma to the soteriological religious template, complete with revealed truths and their custodians – a professional priestly class materially supported by a religiously-dependent laity.

Ñāṇavīra drew out the implications of this view in drastic terms. The Pali commentaries constituted mere 'dead matter', ignorance of which was to be commended in one's deeper study of the canon. In particular, he restored the emphasis, in the putative first discourse of the Buddha, on the four tasks of the practitioner rather than the revelatory 'noble truths': 'they are imperatives, they call for action (like the bottle in *Alice in Wonderland* labelled "Drink Me!").'[55] While Batchelor shows more (selective) respect for later contributors to the tradition such as Nāgārjuna, Shāntideva, and some Zen sages, his own approach owes something to his predecessor's: he bypasses the religious development since the Buddha's death in order to open up a direct channel back to the world of the Pali canon and of its protagonist, Gotama. In particular (as we will see below), he builds on Ñāṇavīra's reworking of the four noble truths.

Having done so, Batchelor – like any other reader – must pick out a coherent discursive thread from the canon's cacophony of contrasting voices, assertions and *obiter dicta*. Crucially, he foregrounds what Gotama has to say that distinguishes his teaching from positions that a Brahmin or a Jain of his time might just as well have announced – positions that merely restate ambient beliefs rather than strike out in a new direction. Having thus isolated what is unique to the Buddha's teaching with this hermeneutic move, Batchelor proceeds to bolster it by picking up resonances with it in western thought. He evokes sympathetic currents in the latter to present the Buddha's awakening as 'an existential readjustment' (p. 129) that is more recognisable and less exotic for his readership, and often to crystallise dharmic conceptions of the human condition.

For example, Heidegger's presentation of it in terms of process (as being-there, being-in-the-world, being-towards-death, being-with-others and so on) rather than an ontological status, can help many to come to grips with key dharmic experiences and concepts such as not-self (*anattā*) and emptiness (*śūnyatā*).

The process that matters above all others in Batchelor's reinterpretation of the Buddha's teaching is *living this very life*. For him the Buddha adumbrated a *practical philosophy* comparable to the foremost ancient Greek thinkers, rather than set himself up as the prophet of a new religion. The dharma addresses the generic questions of all humanist modes of thought: How should I live? What sort of person should I become? Such ethical questions demand answers in a specific historical context.

This primary ethical aspect touches on the meaning Batchelor ascribes to secularity, deriving as it does from the Latin *saeculum* (a particular age or century). 'I think of myself as a secular Buddhist who is concerned entirely with the demands of this age,' he declares in the final paragraph of *Confession* (p. 240). This meaning does not impel him on an anti-religious crusade. Some versions of religion share this emphasis. Indeed, in the previous chapter, we saw Charles Taylor arguing that secularity is an *achievement* of seven centuries of western religious evolution, one that promises a more meaningful religious life.[56] Secularity only takes issue with a religiosity that highlights post-mortem existences, beyond-human transcendence, and timeless truth-claims.

But that issue is a hefty one for conventional Buddhism, focused as it is on the twin goals of favourable rebirth and ultimate transcendence of *dukkha* which – as the Buddha specifies it in the first discourse – encompasses the inevitable difficulties that inhere in human life as such. This conventional emphasis renders dharma practice as a movement towards a destination rather than as a guide to living this present life; and as an individual solution even when being practised communally. In contrast, Batchelor's rendition points dharma practice towards full human flourishing in this life and the nurturing of a communal 'culture of awakening'

– the seeds of a new civilisation, as Trevor Ling suggested decades earlier (pp. 190–191).

Thus Batchelor draws fire from defenders of the old-style religion by quoting the Buddha in ways that demystify its most exalted 'attainments' and bring them within any sincere practitioner's immediate reach. 'Stream entry' stands for heartfelt conversion to the dharma. 'Nirvana' is an accessible, lucid state of mind in which greed, hatred and ignorance have ceased (however momentarily) and is thereby the precondition to serious cultivation of the eightfold path. 'Awakening' comes down to 'a radical shift of perspective' whereby one abandons old habits of mind to root oneself in 'the contingent, transient, ambiguous, unpredictable, fascinating, and terrifying ground called "life"' (pp. 128–129). All this – in the Buddha's own words – is 'clearly visible, immediate, inviting, uplifting, to be personally sensed by the wise'.[57] Gone, then, are the privileged access to esoteric knowledge and revelatory omniscience of the irreversibly Awakened Ones, and the after-death happy landings in dukkha-free realms.

Batchelor draws out the implications of his interpretation for meditation practice. As a Tibetan monk he baulked at ritualistic evocations and visualisations of archetypal bodhisattvas, and as a counterweight even went on a Goenka-style *vipassanā* retreat. The latter left an enduring impression of the value of intensified awareness of psycho-physical experience in real time – a foretaste of the contingent, transient ground of awakening mentioned above. 'Mindfulness focuses entirely on the specific conditions of one's day-to-day experience. It is not concerned with anything transcendent or divine. It serves as an antidote to theism, a cure for sentimental piety, a scalpel for excising the tumour of metaphysical belief' (p. 130).

A later and more powerful influence in the same direction was the central meditation practice into which the Korean Sŏn master Kusan Sunim initiated him: constantly asking oneself, 'What is this?' Thus 'meditation was no longer a matter of becoming proficient in a technique. It was about sustaining a sensibility that encompassed everything I did' (pp. 64–65). Rather than reaching for esoteric certitudes, this practice served an ethos of sceptical not-knowing. As Kusan kept saying: 'When there is great doubt, then there is great awakening' (p. 65).[58]

Confession of a Buddhist atheist breaks a great deal of new ground in making the dharma intelligible and practicable in the west. It rests on firm foundations in Batchelor's depth of scholarship in the Pali canon, certain developments in the dharmic tradition since the Buddha's death, and cognate currents of ancient and modern western thought, as well as his own decades of experience as a monastic and then a lay dharma teacher. He writes elegantly, lucidly, and persuasively. For the most part he maintains a cool, non-polemical tone.

The book is best not judged by its cover (especially its dust jacket), where tonal lapses occur. Why 'a Buddhist *atheist*' when most informed readers would assume that Buddhism has never had a dog in the fight between theists and atheists in the first place? The dust cover awakens further bewilderment with an endorsement from doyen of 'the new atheists', the late Christopher Hitchens, who lays claim to the book as a contribution to 'ethical and scientific humanism, in which lies our only real hope'. This endorsement might have stimulated sales, but it diminishes and misplaces the book. In chapter 14 Batchelor reassures us that he is an 'ironic' atheist only, and by the end (as we have seen) he has come out as a secular Buddhist, which is something else entirely.

After Buddhism

As noted in the previous chapter, 'Buddhism' as word and concept is an early nineteenth-century European coinage which lumped together a variety of institutionalised and ritualised religious observances that, contents unseen, its authors 'discovered' on their wanderings through Asia. The coinage has acquired a new utility in the current age of solemnised social diversity, including religious toleration. Buddhism can appear as a religion like (and beside) any other – with revealed truths, supernatural beliefs and rituals like any other. Its randomly selected, suitably robed representatives can take their place at official celebrations of multiculturalism. In his *After Buddhism*, Batchelor is seeking to retrieve the dharma from *that* conventional Buddhism. He's certainly not leaving the dharma behind, as the subtitle *Rethinking the dharma for a secular age* makes clear.

The main title also implicitly acknowledges a debt to recent Christian thinkers who have sought to distil from their own tradition a navigable ethical path for the present secular age, one couched in a post-metaphysical sensibility – a process that has involved peeling away its supernatural and metaphysical elements. For our purposes, the most prominent of these thinkers is Batchelor's friend Don Cupitt, the academic and former Anglican priest who wrote (beside much else) *After God*.[59] Another who has influenced Batchelor is the Italian still-Catholic philosopher Gianni Vattimo, author of *After Christianity*.[60] So book titles beginning with 'After' go with the territory. In this context it's worth recalling that 'secular Christianity' first announced itself in a book title over a half-century ago.[61]

In this dharmic retrieval, Batchelor seeks to integrate themes in his writings since *Alone with others* (1983), including those in *Confession*. He restates his starting point, not in disinterested academic scholarship, but in the urgent questions that dharma practice itself poses, starting with 'What does it mean to practice the dharma in the context of modernity?' (p. ix). 'As a practicing Buddhist, I look to the discourses not just to mine them for scholarly knowledge but to come to terms with my own birth and death,' he declares in the first synthesising chapter (p. 21).

Unlike *Confession*, this book does not rely on an overarching narrative structure, although it contains poignant narrative content – including reminders of the stages in its author's own development. The structure alternates chapters developing conceptual perspectives with ones that recover the stories of five significant figures in the Buddha's life, three of whom were laymen practising under the Buddha's personal tutelage while dealing with the pressing demands of their vocations in a dangerous world. They are Gotama's cousin Mahānāma, who presided over the Sakiyan council; Gotama's powerful but capricious patron Pasenadi, king of Kosala; and Jīvaka, physician at the Magadhan court.

These individuals, whom the monastic commentators have neglected, have greater relevance to lay western practitioners today than the conventional pantheon of monastic achievers who have 'realised the Goal'. The individual stories also evoke significant issues for dharma practice around 'this great matter of birth and death', such as the formative experience of conversion, and the significance of care (*appamāda*) as the dharma's master virtue. In this way they are singularly moving, while pinpointing spiritual conundrums that still manifest today in several major religious traditions, not to mention our own life-processes.

Thus Batchelor returns us to the heat and dust of Gotama's world, the Ganges basin of the fifth century BCE. But interestingly, he changes canonical horses, no longer relying on the Pali canon, but on the *vinaya* (monastic rule) of the Mūlasarvāstavāda school, preserved in Tibetan and translated into English by the American diplomat and polymath Woodville Rockhill.[62] With little variation, it tells the same story as the Pali canon. These two accounts, Batchelor surmises, drew on the same original version that probably existed between the Buddha's death and the reign of Ashoka in the third century BCE.

He returns to these roots precisely as a *traditionalist* in the sense elaborated by Alasdair MacIntyre, whom he quotes (p. 20): 'A living tradition is an historically extended, socially embodied argument, and an argument...about the goods which constitute that tradition'.[63] As we noted in the previous chapter, such a tradition of practice is thus an intergenerational conversation, which can be sustained only so long as its current practitioners and contributors remain conscious of its origins and generative questions, and the course of the conversation to the present time. MacIntyre goes on to contrast such a living tradition with a dead one in which the current practitioners have no access to its evolutionary trajectory, thus cannot contribute to it, and merely inherit and reproduce the usages of the preceding generation as they stand. Tactfully, Batchelor refrains from explicitly applying this characterisation to conventional Buddhism, but in *Secular Buddhism* he will come close:

> I have long been puzzled why Buddhists of all traditions unhesitatingly describe themselves as followers of the Buddha yet ignore or disparage the discourses that are most likely to go back to him, put into his mouth sayings and views that emerged centuries after his death, regard the mythic account of his life as biography, and accept a comically idealized picture of what he looked like (p. 14).

Batchelor characterises the living dharmic tradition as a life-affirming *task-based ethical path*, a phrase I will expand on below. Early in *After Buddhism* he excludes from it two present-day tendencies: 'a Buddhism that seeks to discard all trace of religiosity, that seeks to arrive at a dharma that is little more than a set of self-help techniques that enable us to operate more calmly and effectively as agents or clients, or both, of capitalist consumerism'; and 'the *secularization* of Buddhism, which renders Buddhist ideas and practices palatable and useful for those who have no interest in committing themselves to the core values of the dharma' (p. 17).

True to his synthesising purpose, Batchelor works into this book a number of themes already canvassed in *Confession* and other writings. To keep this chapter within reasonable limits, I will touch on some salient ideas that appear here for the first time, or in enhanced form – ones which stand out in his original contribution to the dharma today.

To begin with, he completes the transition from the conventional four noble truths – the central beliefs of conventional Buddhism – to 'the fourfold task'. As noted above, on Ñāṇavīra's reading of the first discourse in Pali, the supposed 'noble truths' were actually 'imperatives' to be carried out, rather than revelations and articles of faith.[64] Later, the leading scholar of Prakrit dialects (especially Pali), KR Norman, concluded on syntactical grounds that the term 'noble truth' (*ariya-saccam*) must have been added to the discourse sometime after its original formulation.[65] If we now excise this apparently apocryphal term and fine-tune our translation of the Pali text, Batchelor argues, the first discourse becomes a limpid and coherent recipe for action – an ethical path based on care, one on which one flourishes and fully realises one's human potential as an ethical agent.

Interpreted in this way, the first discourse announces a 'middle way' that steers clear of the two dead ends of infatuation and mortification. It defines this path in terms of four tasks that so tightly follow each other in a sequence that we can usefully roll them into just one task with four aspects. First, one must fully embrace the difficult aspects to which human flesh is heir (*duk-*

kha), which the Buddha specifies as birth, ageing, sickness, death, encountering what is not dear, separation from what is dear, not getting what one wants, and the five bundles of clinging (*khandhas* – aspects of human experience). Second, let go of the reactivity (greed, hatred, and delusion) with which we habitually meet these difficulties and thus actually compound them. Third, behold (register, indeed relish) the experience of a mind state entirely free from reactivity (nirvana). Fourth, so inspired, dedicate oneself to cultivating the eightfold path consisting of appropriate view, intention, speech, action, livelihood, effort, mindfulness, and mental integration. While the four tasks are sequential, in practice they are coterminous; they enhance each other, so constituting a lifelong feedback loop.

A second salient theme in *After Buddhism* is the rejection of the correspondence theory of truth that underpins dogma, metaphysical truth-claims in general, and conventional Buddhist beliefs in particular (pp. 117–120). According to this theory – equally at home in popular culture as in learned discourse – truth-claims can be tested against some sort of ultimate reality or metaphysics. Batchelor quotes many instances of the Buddha refusing to answer metaphysical questions, criticising the way metaphysical arguments distract from practice focused on one's immediate predicament, and counselling against attachment to views. '[T]he word "truth" (*sacca*) in the Pali discourses predominantly refers to the virtue of being truthful, honest, loyal, and sincere,' Batchelor comments (pp. 117–8). In modern English we retain this ethical usage in expressions like 'a true friend'. Ethical truth appears to be the only truth that the Buddha dealt in.

On this point Batchelor makes common cause with modern post-metaphysical thinkers. For the pragmatists, as for the Buddha, a truth-claim should be judged by its usefulness to human wellbeing, not its supposed correspondence with some ultimate reality. It will, in any event, only ever amount to an interpretation that depends on our agreement to make it appear to be 'true' in some ultimate sense (p. 119). When people believe themselves to be in (exclusive) possession of the Truth, especially religious truth, they have proven capable of waging war and committing genocide to assert it. In this context, Batchelor quotes Gianni Vattimo in *A farewell to truth*: 'When the word "truth" is uttered, a shadow of violence is cast as well'.[66] This critique of metaphysical truth subverts the central truth-claims of conventional Buddhism – rebirth and the four noble truths – while reinforcing Batchelor's characterisation of the dharma as a task-based ethical path which requires no support in metaphysical constructs.

A third major theme developed in *After Buddhism* touches on 'the everyday sublime' as a meditative experience and a key facet of the sensibility that dharma practice fosters. In a striking passage, its author declares:

> Meditation originates and culminates in the everyday sublime. I have little interest in achieving states of sustained concentration in which the sensory richness of experience is replaced by pure introspective rapture. I have no interest in reciting mantras, visualizing Buddhas or mandalas, gaining out-of-body experiences, reading other people's thoughts, practicing lucid dreaming, or channeling psychic energies through chakras, let alone letting my consciousness be absorbed in the transcendent perfection of the Unconditioned. Meditation is about embracing what is happening to this organism as it touches its environment in this moment. I do not reject the experience of the mystical. I reject only the view that the mystical is concealed behind what is merely apparent, that it is anything other than what is occurring in time and space right now. The mystical does

not transcend the world but saturates it. 'The mystical is not how the world is', noted Ludwig Wittgenstein in 1921, 'but that it is' (p. 231).

Implicitly Batchelor is foregrounding Zen and insight meditation practice – the two Buddhist traditions that have gone furthest in penetrating today's western culture. They also accommodate the kind of non-technical approaches to meditation that would align with his perspective.[67]

He is also embracing numinous experience and the radical shifts in consciousness that can arise in intense practice of these disciplines, and at other moments in our lives when we focus fully on the flow of our immediate being-there. Without being grounded in the everyday sublime, these experiences otherwise default into culturally established transcendental beliefs that sever them from their origins in the actual texture of our lives. The reference to the 'everyday' implicitly evokes the 'average everydayness' that reverberates throughout Heidegger's *Being and time*. The 'sublime' explicitly references Edmund Burke's youthful 1757 work *The sublime and the beautiful*, and the Romantic poets. Burke, Heidegger and Batchelor are all evoking experiences that are so mysterious, and bafflingly beautiful or terrifying, that they beggar our capacity to represent them in words or images. If we plunge deeply enough into any moment of our experience – this 'groundless ground' in Zen terms – it will reveal itself as sublime in this sense. In Batchelor's presentation, awakening to the everyday sublime constitutes a vital facet of the awakening process itself.

Batchelor renders a key canonical formulation of the Buddha's awakening as follows:

This dharma I have reached is deep, hard to see, difficult to awaken to, quiet and excellent, not confined to thought, subtle, sensed by the wise. But people love their place...: they delight and revel in their place. It is hard for people who love, delight, and revel in their place to see this ground..., 'because-of-this' conditionality.... And also hard to see this ground: the stilling of inclinations, the relinquishing of bases, the fading away of reactivity, desirelessness, ceasing, nirvana (pp. 333–334).[68]

Here awakening appears as a drastic change of existential perspective from habitual attachments and ways of life (*habitus*, Pierre Bourdieu might say) to an intense experience of our conditions of existence: the groundless ground of contingency in total flux, but one in which the boon of nirvana – a mind state free of habitual reactivity – is always accessible. Hence the vital experiences of conditionality and nirvana constitute the process of awakening, not esoteric knowledge, let alone omniscience.

As we'll see in chapter 7, in Peter Watson's survey of post-metaphysical western thinkers and creative writers (from Heidegger to Proust, and many in between) the common thread that brings them together is the ideal of living *intensely*.[69] In plain terms: this life is no mere rehearsal for the next – it's the main event, the only life we will ever have. So we need to live it to the full, with urgency, intensity, and authenticity. With his concept of the everyday sublime, Batchelor brings dharma practice further into alignment with this late-modern ethos.

Secular Buddhism

Whereas *After Buddhism* develops around a carefully constructed argument, my first impression of *Secular Buddhism* was that it constitutes a companion volume (in smaller format) to both the former and *Confession*. Among other things, it reproduces in their original form some of Batchelor's essays going back to the mid-

1990s, ones which enlarge upon the turning points he describes in *Confession*. But as usual, first impressions deceive. Apart from being a self-described 'scholar-practitioner' (p. 4), he's a practising artist in two disciplines – photography and collage – the aesthetics and dharmic relevance of which he discusses in the final section of the book. The intricate, five-part structure of *Secular Buddhism* in fact draws on collage principles.

The constituent parts in turn unfurl Ñāṇavīra's contribution, and his life sympathetically recalled in the round; a summation of how secular Buddhism diverges from the conventional version; a miscellany of controversial topics (starting with rebirth); recorded key conversations with others; and desiderata for a Buddhist aesthetics. (To follow him into this latter territory would require a separate chapter. Suffice it to say that he is here initiating a project to make good the underdevelopment of the aesthetic dimension in historical Buddhism and its culture.) The contents of each part follow a chronological order and thereby support the narrative of the author's own spiritual evolution.

There is an overarching third artistic project at work here: the author's search for a 'voice' in the writerly sense – an idiom in which to convey not only his own spiritual ideals, doubts, and inquiries, but also to express canonical insights in ways that lend them wings in a modern sensibility. Overall, this book takes us backstage, to show how the more public Stephen Batchelor has come to present his major performances on stage (as it were), and what we might expect from him in the future.

The book contains surprises, too. Perhaps the biggest of them consists in his spirited defence of the spread of therapeutic mindfulness (pp. 166–9), coming as it does after his dismissal of secularising, stand-alone self-help techniques based on extrapolations from Buddhism (quoted above under '*After Buddhism*'). In fact, he contributed to the British all-party parliamentary inquiry into the subject. In its report, *Mindful nation UK*, it recommended the deployment of mindfulness training in major areas of social practice: health, workplaces, criminal justice, and education.[70] The National Health Service now funds mindfulness training for people suffering from mental-health issues that it has been shown to alleviate. Mindfulness practice goes to the heart of the dharma, he argues; it's the seventh path factor, after all. Buddhists should not gainsay this major inroad of the culture of awakening into the functioning of a core western society. Among the many thousands that mindfulness now touches will be some who will feel the urge to trace it back to the dharma itself.

'A secular Buddhism', an essay Batchelor first published in 2012, constitutes the second section of the book, as well as its crux. It sets out to delineate his version of secular Buddhism in contrast to the conventional version in all its apparently divergent forms. He does so by building on an analogy with operating systems in the world of computers. Conventional Buddhism becomes Buddhism 1.0, an operating system that supports the many different 'programmes' of which institutionalised Buddhism consists, from the Theravāda through the Mahāyāna to the various strains of Tibetan Buddhism. But secular-Buddhist insights and practices call for a new operating system, Buddhism 2.0 (pp. 79–81). Before computers invaded our lives, we used to call conceptual leaps of this magnitude *paradigm shifts* in honour of Thomas Kuhn, or even *epistemological breaks* à la Louis Althusser.

Buddhism 1.0 supports a soteriological religion that requires adherence to a belief system. It promises individual salvation and transcendence based on fidelity to a multi-life perspective (rebirth) and the four noble truths understood as revealed truths. The form of transcendence it offers is full awakening, which permanently removes the practitioner from the suffering endemic to the human condition and reveals ultimate truths inaccessible to the unawakened. Maintenance of Buddhism 1.0's subsidiary programmes calls for a professional priestly class and their hierarchical monastic institutions as repositories of doctrine, spiritual authority, and ritual. The Buddha himself manifests as an historically decontextualised, beyond-human, protean figure to whom can be ascribed whatever doctrines (including post-Gotama canonical texts) emerge from monastic institutions and their luminaries.

In contrast, Buddhism 2.0 supports a task-based ethical path that does not rest on any belief system, promise of salvation or transcendence, and promotes a single-life perspective. That path starts with the fourfold task (or 'the four great tasks') specified in the first discourse, including the eightfold path itself. It points the way to human flourishing and moral agency, in the first instance at the individual level, but also as the basis of an emerging culture of awakening that has civic ramifications. At both levels awakening is a process rather than a change of status; it involves neither access to special knowledge nor a terminus in some post-human existence.

Secular Buddhism's criterion of truth is an ethical one premised on human wellbeing; Buddhism 2.0 does not support metaphysical truth-claims. Communal practice and realisation are vital, and must proceed from inclusive and egalitarian forms of association rather than exclusive and hierarchical ones. The Buddha was a human being – like anyone else, he was a child of his time and place. His teachings can only be understood in their historical context; to be effective they need to be adapted to each new age and cultural milieu that receives them.

The contrast here is striking, especially given that both paradigms proceed from the same teaching, starting with the Buddha's first discourse. Many other teachings spawn divergent interpretations in Batchelor's work as well. Perhaps he could have reduced the friction between them by more firmly nailing down his hermeneutic approach. He does aver that 'each generation has the right and duty to reinterpret the teachings that it has inherited. In doing so we may discover meanings in these texts that speak lucidly to our own *saeculum* but of which the original authors and their successors may have been unaware' (81). This statement, and Batchelor's general approach to interpreting the canon, lead me to suspect that Hans-Georg Gadamer in particular has influenced his work more than somewhat. If explicitly introduced, the latter's hermeneutics might have contributed to the authority of Batchelor's interpretations and undercut his critics' quest for the timelessly 'correct' way to read the canon.

He could have gone further in his comparison of Buddhist operating systems by contrasting their end users as well. Buddhism 1.0 underpins a mass institutionalised religion that infuses folkways and whole societies in many parts of Asia and their diasporic offshoots in the west, whereas Buddhism 2.0 in the first instance supports small-scale urban practice communities and their websites in the west. Nonetheless, he does acknowledge the gulf between these two sets of end users in the circumstance that, from the late 1960s, 'Buddhism was catapulted into modernity from deeply conservative, agrarian societies in Asia' (159).

One of Batchelor's favourite pragmatist philosophers, Richard Rorty, might have helped him to sharpen the contrast between his operating systems still further by reference to his own two opposing models of ethical aspiration: self-purification as against self-enlargement. Ascetic monastic training under the auspices of Buddhism 1.0 gravitates towards the former: the desire 'to slim down, to peel away everything that is accidental,...to become a simpler and more transparent being'. For instance (as noted in the previous chapter), the fifth-century CE Pali commentary that underpins the orthodox Theravāda is appropriately entitled *The path of purification*. The self-purification model evokes the angels of the Christian imaginary and the fully awakened beings of the conventional Buddhist one. In contrast, Buddhism 2.0 inclines towards self-enlargement: 'the desire to embrace more and more possibilities, to be constantly learning, to give oneself entirely over to curiosity, to end by having embraced all the possibilities of the past and the future'.[71]

Do we have to take a definitive position for or against transcendence, as the choice between operating systems suggests? In the previous chapter we saw Martha Nussbaum mounting a powerful argument against the aspiration to transcend the human condition in a perfection and immortality alien to us – what she calls 'external transcendence'. Instead she holds out the prospect of an 'internal transcendence' – a gradual transition 'to a kind of precision of feeling and thought that a human being can cultivate', the 'fine-tuned perception and bewildered human grace' achievable in our current lives.[72] With these words she seems to clinch the vision that Batchelor offers us, and does so in a way that allows us to retain our being-towards-death decency while pursuing the project of becoming so much more than we already are.

For the benefit of the time-poor reader, I had hoped to end this chapter by ranking the three books under review according to their importance. I now find this hope to be beyond reach. They share the virtue of elegant, clear and coherent writing, but they come into their shared subject matter from different angles, to end up together presenting a cubist whole that is more than the sum of its parts. The intractably time-poor reader will thus have to choose which part she or he wants most – the narrative of Batchelor's formation in *Confession*; the more formal argumentation of *After Buddhism*, or the collage-like *Secular Buddhism*. After reading any one of these books, s/he might find their time-poverty less constraining than at first thought, and come back for more.

Mainstream Buddhists – and non-Buddhists who cleave to mainstream assumptions about what Buddhism is – will find at least some of the contents of these books unfamiliar, even jarring. In which case it is well to remember John Maynard Keynes's insight in the last sentence of the preface to his ground-breaking work, *The general theory of employment, interest and money*: 'The difficulty lies, not in the new ideas, but in escaping from the old ones, which ramify, for those brought up as most of us have been, into every corner of our minds.'[73]

Do we really need to escape from the old ideas? The main manifestations of Buddhism in the west today are simply Asian transplants, with or without the adoption of local languages and other ready-to-hand surface modifications. The deeper acculturation of the dharma to the modern west has barely begun. It will require all those involved to face the issues that Stephen Batchelor raises in the three books under review.

One issue he does not raise touches on the viability of his conception of secular Buddhism as the basis of resilient sangha- and movement-building – the precondition to his 'culture of awakening'. He presents Gotama's dharma as a *practical philosophy* (a philosophy that supports a practice and way of life), a familiar category in classical Greek and Roman civilisation. And he strongly suggests that it should now be reissued in the west as a practical philosophy rather than a religion. But why did the dharma morph into a religion so quickly after Gotama's death, and how compelling is even the most persuasive practical philosophy under late-modern conditions?

In his classic work, *The varieties of religious experience*, the pragmatist philosopher William James evaluates religions precisely on the use-value (in terms of human welfare) of various kinds of personal religious experience.[74] With their offers of solace, certitudes, ecstatic moments, life-after-death and external transcendence, religions tend to out-compete practical philosophies on the market in experiences to assuage the discomforts and insecurity of the human condition. In this way, James argues, religions as social phenomena can outlive any amount of scepticism towards their doctrinal premises, even among their active adherents. Perhaps this circumstance helps explain the dharma's rapid metamorphosis into a religion after the founder's death. Perhaps it also sounds a warning about secular Buddhism's prospects for attracting a committed mass following now. After all, this doctrine encourages clear-eyed embrace of human anguish, insecurity and finitude, not their blurring or deflection.

Buddhism shows no sign of becoming a mass movement among ethnic westerners in any of its manifestations. For the reasons James adduces, many of those who are nevertheless drawn to it seem to prefer the religious experiences that Buddhism 1.0 offers, embellished by the orientalist frisson of the Asian transplants. But in this secular age, a more formidable competitor looms over both religion and practical philosophy on the market in palliative experiences: the psych disciplines, now including those that purvey therapeutic mindfulness.

Our individualistic 'age of authenticity' since the 1960s, Charles Taylor suggests, comes with an anti-communitarian ethos that discourages mobilisation in practice communities, whether religious or philosophical.[75] An important attraction of the psych disciplines, including the mindfulness-based ones, is their adaptation to this ethos. Their services come packaged and commodified as one-on-one consultations, or courses of fixed duration; their purveyors are accredited professionals who take a fee for service; their products promise achievement of explicit personal goals, and boast evidence-based outcomes. No sociability, volunteering, civic virtue or open-ended commitment to evening meetings is called for; nor any ethical undertakings. To access the boons in question, the individual has only to pay the entry fee.

The dharma points to a human potential that goes far beyond enabling us 'to operate more calmly and effectively as agents or clients, or both, of capitalist consumerism', as Stephen Batchelor puts it in an earlier quote. Despite the strength of his work in reframing that potential in a way that draws on leading thinkers of our own time and culture, he is still swimming against the individualistic adaptive stream that the psych disciplines exemplify. But then again, Gotama applied that same metaphor to his own awakening process.

However, today we face an existential threat to our species (among others) in the form of human-induced global warming. It can only be met by our species' coordinated effort to radically change the principles and institutions that govern us and are driving us towards the destruction of life as we know it. The increasingly acknowledged need for collective and co-ordinated action may awaken us from our individualistic torpor – a matter I will return to in Part V of this book.

Chapter 3

Secular Buddhism: scientistic versus interpretive

The secular-Buddhist movement has barely announced its name before seemingly risking incoherence by breaking down into two divergent tendencies. What seems to be the dominant one in the USA aligns with scientistic atheism and the recent claims of the life sciences (especially neuroscience), and spends a lot of time debunking beliefs and prejudices associated with Abrahamic monotheism. Yet both Abrahamic religion and science play the same *language game*, as Wittgenstein would say – they speak in *revelations*. It's a point I'll return to. The other secular-Buddhist tendency, found mainly in the rest of the English-speaking world, abandons the language of revelation altogether, be it Abrahamic or scientistic, in favour of post-metaphysical, interpretive language, that is, a first-person discourse arising out of the conscious experience of engaged human agents.

Let's provisionally call these tendencies of secular Buddhism *scientistic* and *interpretive* respectively. And let's note that the geographical division is no accident. US society exhibits qualitatively higher rates of Abrahamic belief and religious adherence than other western societies, so here 'that ole-time religion', mischievously enough, retains a lot of cultural prestige and political clout. For instance, one of Donald Trump's rusted-on constituencies consists of evangelical Christians. Thus it's no wonder an atheism industry has grown up in the USA to deal with the problem.

In the wider west, by contrast, unreconstructed Abrahamic

religions have lost prestige and political clout to the point where their adherents don't really bother the rest of us any more. And post-metaphysical thought seems to provide a much closer fit with the Buddha's own teaching. Moreover, some of us are making friends with progressive Christians who, by and large, have been speaking our post-metaphysical, interpretive language longer than Buddhists have.

How the tension plays out in western philosophy

The nascent scientistic/interpretive divide within secular Buddhism also coincides with the sectarian fissure separating the Anglo-American or 'analytic' wing of western philosophy from the 'Continental' one. Brutally summarised, the first of these pursues *knowledge* in the form of truth-claims, and prioritises metaphysics and epistemology; whereas the second pursues *wisdom* and embraces such post-metaphysical schools as phenomenology, existentialism and pragmatism.[76]

The analytic wing upholds the necessity of an 'objective' view-from-nowhere (or God's-eye-view) and the truth claims – both religious and scientific – that it spawns. It sees language as mirroring (representing) ultimate realities, and so capable of expressing something called 'truth'. The post-metaphysical, interpretive schools, by contrast, focus on *the perceptions of situated agents*, and see language as 'anti-representational' or 'non-realist' – as a tool for expressing and achieving human needs and interests, not as a mirror to objective reality. In this second case, speech acts can be more or less useful (just like other tools – saucepans, screwdrivers, aeroplanes, etc.), but not 'true' or 'false'. Utility trumps truth. And interpretation – hermeneutics – can enhance the productiveness (usefulness) of speech acts, as Gianni Vattimo suggests.[77]

Take the most obvious example of the divergence in question: the God problem, which sells so many books at airports. In

Anglo-American/analytic vein, atheists have battled theists for decades over whether s/he/it exists or not as an objective reality. From a post-metaphysical perspective, though, the questions would rather concern when the God metaphor arose, whose needs and interests it served, and whether it has remained useful or been creatively repurposed.

In the late nineteenth century Friedrich Nietzsche, and then the pragmatist philosopher John Dewey, suggested that God was now a dead metaphor, one that had outlived its usefulness, and should be laid to rest with all the other dead metaphors. This is what Nietzsche's notorious phrase 'God is dead' announced: the death of a metaphor. He was not promoting atheism, which – just like theism – proposes an 'objective' truth-claim divorced from needs and interests. This debate over whether God exists or not leaves the engaged human agent none the wiser. Secular Buddhists, I'm suggesting, should avoid entering the lists in jousts like this – debates that lead nowhere and don't concern us.

By now it'll be clear that I cleave to post-metaphysical, interpretive wing of secular Buddhism.

The travails of scientism

As I suggested in my first chapter, one of Buddhism's first selling points in the west in the late nineteenth century was its supposed status as a 'scientific religion' in two senses: it did not resist evolutionary biology as Christianity did; and it shared a research object – the human mind – with that other emerging glamour science of the time, psychology.

Then as now, scientistic publicists seemed strangely unaware of empirical science's origins in western Christianity: it began as 'natural philosophy' with a remit to study nature as a way of understanding how the Creator's mind worked, something that could be read off natural phenomena closely observed. So science learned the language game of revelation on its progenitor's knee. But having forgotten its own origins, science has declared war on its parent, now its competitor on the revelation market.

Buddhism's love affair with western natural science has waxed and waned since it first received the accolade of 'scientific religion'. But now it's waxing again around neuroscience, genetics and genomics, once more on the basis of a supposedly shared interest in the human mind. The findings of these now heavily commercialised branches of science are contested, but also hyped and oversold, often with Buddhists' help.

Steven Poole comments: *'We have outsourced the job of interpreting ourselves to the modern life sciences.'*[78] He thus makes a crucial point and sounds a dire warning, not least to Buddhists. One way of understanding the thrust of the earliest Buddhist teachings is that they're precisely about the work of experiential self-interpretation as the royal road to assuming self-responsibility, and they eschew metaphysical revelations as a diversion from this practice.[79] As against that dharmic thrust, a typically religious move consists in infantilising us by depriving us of 'the job of interpreting ourselves'. Priests do it, gurus do it, and now celebrity scientists do it.

Misunderstand me correctly (as the Swedes say). I find the more hard-nosed findings of neuroscience – to take that example – fascinating. They embellish the wallpaper of my cognitive life, my reality construct. My own favourite celebrity neuroscientist – Susan Greenfield – also sends us an important ethical message based on her discipline.[80] No doubt others do so too.

But ambivalence arises when I recognise yet another round of biological determinism, yet another clockwork-orange moment, one more attempt to foist a reductionist framework onto us, simplifying us so as to obviate once and for all the intricate work of interpreting ourselves afresh every day, and without presuppositions.

Post-metaphysical secularism does not crusade against religion as such (still less against science), only against manifestations of religion and science that pretend to be true in a way that short-circuits our self-interpretation. Aspects of both religion and science continue to prove useful in serving human needs and interests, including informing-without-disabling our work of self-interpretation. Let's by all means engage with them, then. But with our eyes wide open, and Karl Marx's question – *Cui bono?* (Who benefits?) – on our lips.

Notes

1 2007: 21.

2 Bubna-Litic and Higgins 2007.

3 For example, Wallace 2010.

4 Taylor 1989 and 2007.

5 Taylor 2007: 18.

6 Bechert 1966. C.f. Lopez's (2002), 'modern Buddhism'.

7 Gombrich and Obeyesekere 1988.

8 See Lopez 2008.

9 Burnouf [1844] 2010.

10 McMahan 2008.

11 Woodhead and Heelas 2000; McMahan 2008; Taylor 1989.

12 Gombrich and Obeyesekere 1988.

13 Nārada 1979; Buddhaghosa 1956.

14 Taylor 2007: 159–171.

15 McMahan 2008; Woodhead and Heelas 2000.

16 McMahan 2008: 52–3, following Woodhead and Heelas 2000; Safran 2003.

17 Carrette and King 2005; Dawson and Turnbull 2006; Purser 2019.

18 Magid 2008.

19 E.g., Wallace 2010.

20 MacIntyre 1985: 146, 222–25.

21 See for example Tambiah 1992. Umberto Eco's novel *The name of the rose* (2004), set in a fourteenth-century Catholic monastery, dramatises these power-full processes in monasteries, including the use of theology as a power resource in political conflict.

22 Foucault 1977 and 1980. See also Voyce 2017.

23 Ñaṇavīra Thera [1965] 2001.

24 Siff 2010: 146–7 and passim.

25 Leader 2009: 2, 18.

26 See Mishra 2004 and Batchelor 2010, building on earlier accounts, such as Ling 1973: 43-129.

27 Pocock 2006.

28 C.f. Kuzminski 2008.

29 Vattimo 2002: 62–3.

30 Taylor 2007: 1–3.

31 Taylor 2006.

32 Taylor 2007: 61.

33 For instance Geering 1992.

34 Weber [1905] 2001.

35 Vattimo 2002: 26, 98.

36 Ñāṇavīra Thera [1965] 2001 and Batchelor 1983.

37 Bellah 1970: ch. 9.

38 Taylor 2007: 473–504.

39 Faure 2009.

40 Taylor 2007: 19–20.

41 See Owen Flanagan's (2011) discussion of 'eudaimonia Buddha' from a neuro-philosophical viewpoint.

42 Douglas [1966] 1976: 161. Richard Rorty (1991: 154) captures these alternative visions of human development in his contrast between 'a search for purity' on the one hand, and one for 'self-enlargement' on the other. I expand on this point in ch. 9.

43 Lasch 1979; Twenge and Campbell 2009.

44 Nussbaum 1990: 365–391.

45 Nussbaum 1990: 379; her emphasis.

46 Nussbaum 1990: 381; her emphasis.

47 Heidegger [1927] 2008: 279–311; Vattimo 2002: 134; Mercier 2008.

48 Ñāṇavīra Thera [1965] 2001; Heidegger [1927] 2008; Batchelor 1983.

49 Merleau-Ponty 1962 and 1968.

50 Ñāṇamoli [1972] 2001.

51 Malalasekera [1938] 1997; Ling 1973.

52 Together with Martine Batchelor he has taken to teaching residential retreats based on Sŏn meditation at Gaia House. See Batchelor & Batchelor 2019.

53 Ñāṇavīra's writings were first published in 1987 in *Clearing the path* (Ñāṇavīra, [1987] 2001), twenty-two years after his death, and came to Batchelor's attention in 1989.

54 Recently Martin Hägglund (2020) has eloquently insisted on our acknowledge-ment of the finality of death if we are to live meaningfully in what he calls 'secular faith', as we'll see in chapter 5.

55 Ñāṇavira [1987] 2001: 106–107. The discourse in question is the Dhammacak-kapavattana sutta: *Samyutta nikāya* 56:11.

56 Taylor 2007.

57 *Aṅguttara nikāya* VI: 47, quoted in Batchelor 2015: 340.

58 Martine and Stephen Batchelor have illustrated how a retreat based on this practice in a western milieu proceeds today in Batchelor and Batchelor 2019.

59 Cupitt 1997.

60 Vattimo 2002.

61 Smith 1966.

62 Rockhill 1884.

63 MacIntyre 1985: 222.

64 The first commentator to notice the incongruity was apparently Woodward

([1930] 1993: 358n.

65 Norman [1982] 2003: 223.

66 Vattimo 2011: 77.

67 For instance Magid 2008 and Siff 2010.

68 Ariyapariyesanā sutta, *Majjhima nikāya* 26.

69 Watson 2014. C.f. Hägglund 2020 and chapter 5.

70 MAPPG 2015. Batchelor's contribution to it is acknowledged at p. 82.

71 Rorty 1991: 154. I will return to this point in ch. 9.

72 Nussbaum 1990: 365–391. Quotes on p. 379.

73 Keynes, 1936: 5.

74 James [1902] 1994.

75 Taylor 2007: 473–504. I gloss his discussion of this period and its predecessors in the previous chapter.

76 Critchley 2001: ch. 1. Appropriately enough, this chapter bears the title, 'The gap between knowledge and wisdom'.

77 Vattimo 2002: 62–3.

78 Poole 2013 – a review of Rose 2012.

79 However, Owen Flanagan (2011) – who explicitly identifies with analytic philosophy – presents Buddhism as a metaphysics, an epistemology and an ethics. In spite of this, he offers a sophisticated and useful critique of Buddhism's and neuroscience's current flirtation.

80 Especially in Greenfield 2008.

Part II
Western affinities

Introduction to part II

The talks and articles in this part spring from my interest in finding affinities with the dharma and its practice in the western tradition, ancient and modern. Exploring these affinities makes the dharma more familiar and less exotic for ethnic westerners, at the same time as it helps us to articulate points of dharma in fresh and insightful ways.

The following chapter introduces Martin Heidegger's presentation (in his 1927 magnum opus, *Being and time*) of the human person as *process* – as 'being-there' and 'being-in-the-world' in the first instance – rather than as a stable, static *entity*. His work thus enriches the Buddhist meditator's experience of not-self (*anattā*). More generally, it crystallises the implicit account of what it means to be human that arises from the Buddha's most comprehensive teaching on insight meditation, the *Satipaṭṭhāna sutta*.

One essential facet of being-human, Heidegger suggests, is being-towards-death. For him the ever-present sense of the inevitability and finality of our death constitutes an important criterion for living authentically. We are finite beings who need to acknowledge our finitude in order to grasp our situation and make the most of our lives. Finitude has become a major trope in modern western philosophy, and the Swedish writer Martin Hägglund has recently enriched it in his *This life: secular faith and spiritual freedom*. I pick up its relevance to secular dharma in chapter 5.

Hägglund criticises *religious faith* (including conventional Buddhism) for denying the finality of death and focusing faith and spiritual practice on the prospect of a better life after death. This focus devalues – and sometimes even disparages – the spiritual freedom and worldly attachments that underpin our flourishing in *this* life. As against this often passionate pursuit of salvation in the hereafter associated with religious faith, he proposes an equally passionate *secular faith* in the projects and values that imbue our one and only time-bound life with significance. As at-risk, time-bound beings, we pursue values that belong in our world and share our characteristics.

Just as death is the flipside of life, life-denial is the flipside of death-denial. Only by working towards the horizon of our own death can we grasp the possibilities of this life. Major processes in any human life – old age, sickness, and the loss of those closest to us, for instance – are inevitably painful (as the Buddha also noted in his first discourse), but if we dedicate our spiritual lives to evading them, as conventional Buddhism prescribes, we're retreating from the only life we'll ever have.

This argument chimes with Sigmund Freud's work on our responses to transience, in particular how we mourn our dead and other all-important elements of our life that are snatched away from us. I take up this convergence in chapter 6. The very title of Freud's famous essay in this area, 'Mourning and melancholia', names the choice we face when these losses (usually our biggest psychic disruptions) overtake us. We can either undertake the long 'unpleasant work' of mourning, or we can evade it – perhaps in the name of avoiding suffering – by sinking into an effective melancholia. In short, we can either mourn the dead or join them. The former is the way to a restored and enhanced flourishing as we emerge from the mourning process as deeper individuals.

Chapter 7 looks at a survey of the possibilities that

Hägglund's 'secular faith and spiritual freedom' open up. Since Friedrich Nietzsche announced the death of God in 1882, a whole literature has arisen to re-pose in this-worldly terms the question: what gives our lives meaning? Practising insight meditation as the Buddha expounds it leads us to intensify our experience of being alive in aid of cultivating a highly engaged and responsible way of being in the world – a project that many and varied western thinkers have now joined. Peter Watson surveys these contributions in his 2014 book *The age of atheists: how we have sought to live since the death of God,* so he'll prove useful in this context.

Revamp: *writings on secular Buddhism*

Chapter 4

Heidegger, not-self and being-there

Maybe you've heard the not uncommon observation – with which I agree – that the dharma amounts to applied radical phenomenology. The latter is a rather diverse school of modern philosophy, so I'll narrow my comments down to address its main exponent, Martin Heidegger – the grandfather of phenomenology and existentialism. The aspect of Heidegger's thought I'm referring to comes in his magnum opus, *Being and time*, published in German in 1927.[1]

Heidegger felt that western philosophy had got off on the wrong foot in assuming that the experienced world was made up of enduring self-sufficient entities, starting with human beings. Humans thus came to be understood as independent entities – the thinkers and doers (that is, *'subjects'*) who do and know things in, with, to and about other living and/or inanimate entities (all considered as *objects*).

If you think about existence in these terms, Heidegger writes, then you produce misleading ideas about how we humans engage with life and experience it. These ideas skew the way we think about ourselves and the world around us, and how we act in it. We are *not* fixed entities – we are dynamic chains of events or processes. This is the biggest idea I'll try to leave you with in this chapter. But it's not a new one. This is how the Buddha saw things, too.

A more dynamic sense of being human

Heidegger avoided the whole idea of the human person as an en-during entity. Instead he replaced her/him with two almost synonymous concepts: *being-there* or *being-here (Dasein)* and *being-in-the-world (In-der-Welt-sein)*. Both refer to a chain of events, or processes. In English-language discussions of Heidegger, Dasein is usually left untranslated, as any translation doesn't quite convey what is going on here.

To repeat: Heidegger is saying that humans are more *event-like* (or happening-like) than entity-like. Our life process is insepa-rable from our ever-changing surroundings and contexts – whom and what we care about, how we go about our projects, and what happens to us. We don't exist *essentially*, that is, independently of all these life processes.

We're not static bodies existing in glass cases! And we don't learn about stuff by going to school and reading books about them! We come to self-awareness and learn about life by being '*always already*' fully engaged in life. Eternal truths and revelations have no place in this picture.

Each of us is haphazardly '*thrown into*' a particular life-world (a specific family, culture, linguistic community, class, moment in history, etc.) which is *always already* our unchosen world, and in time we '*project' ourselves* out at it in our 'concernful' activities. (Note that the word 'project', too, refers to throwing.)

A recurring expression of Heidegger's is '*average everyday-ness*' – this is where we must be able to account for our lives within the worlds in which we've already been thrown, and then make our own. What are we doing and what are we understanding as we go through a normal day in this personal world of ours – especially before we start to verbalise and theorise about it?

A favourite image for this kind of *being* ('being' understood as a verb rather than a noun) is the artisan – a traditional cobbler, for example – in his workshop. His tools of trade and raw materials are at his fingertips, *'ready-to-hand'*. He doesn't have to think about them as he works with them, they're integral to his own will and body – his being-in-the-world. While at work he's indistinguishable from them and the work he's doing. It doesn't make sense to understand this artisan independently of his workshop and what he's doing and using. He's a process playing itself out.

So this is a much more dynamic picture of how we live, and who and what we are, at any particular moment.

And Heidegger elaborates it. What drives this process (which is us) is what we *care about*: our projects keep us moving forward, engaging with our world, and with other Daseins we rub up against in particular ways. We don't exist as static, semi-permanent essences independently of this engagement. The Buddha saw care (*appamāda*) as the primal ethic of the dharma; Heidegger saw care (*Sorge* in German) as the core dynamic element in our authentic being-in-the-world.

Authenticity and our existential givens

A human life is a trajectory as well as a process. We're all going to die, so Heidegger invents a term for that, too: we're always *'being-towards-death'*. (You gotta love dem hyphens!) Constant awareness of this aspect of our being is in fact one of his two criteria for living *authentically*: engaging with the world always mindful that the engagement itself is finite, and that our possibilities for realising our projects – what we *care* about – are finite too (limited by our lifespan, our energies, our talents, and our real-world opportunities and contingencies).

This idea of authenticity puts a powerful brake on childish and narcissistic grandiosity. It's been preserved in the concept of *finitude* (*Endlichkeit* in German) – something we'll return to in the next chapter. Let me just suggest here that constant awareness of our personal finitude is the touchstone of sanity, and no dharma practitioner should leave home without it.

Heidegger's second criterion for authentic living is resisting social expectations – what he calls 'the they' (*das Man*), as in: '*They* expect me to get a good job, buy a house, get married, and raise a family.' To live authentically, we need to insist on our own priorities, no matter how much pressure is put on us to conform to social expectations.

Heidegger and the dharma

This whole conception of being human chimes in with (and articulates) the Buddha's, and the way our lives appear to us in insight meditation practice – what the Buddha called 'embodied attention' (*yoniso manasikāra*). The only real difference between the Buddha's account and Heidegger's is that the Buddha couched our lack of entity-like status in negative terms, whereas Heidegger accounts for our true event-like being in positive terms. The two accounts are two sides of the same coin.

In insight meditation, one of the three characteristics in every experience that we encounter is our old friend, *anattā* – often mistranslated as 'no-self', which in turn invites unhelpful metaphysical speculation about whether the self 'exists' or not. The Pali word actually means *not-self*: it's not denying the existence of the self as a chain of events or happenings, but it is pointing to the fact that we can't *find* a solid entity-like self in any aspect of our experience when we pay close attention to it. Later dharmic developments elaborated not-self into the meditative realisation of *emptiness* (*śūnyatā*), referring to emptiness-of-self, where self is understood as an enduring entity.

Our life (and experiences that constitute it) arise and pass away – they're event-like, not entity-like, hence 'empty' of self. We can't find a self in any solid, identifiable aspect of our being,

72

because that's just not how we exist anyway. We are the process, not the solid bits; that's how we're to get to know ourselves and how our lives are unfolding. As the third-century CE sage Nāgārjuna put it:

> Were mind and matter me,
> I would come and go like them.
> If I were something else,
> They would say nothing about me.

So quite pragmatically, the Buddha directs our meditative attention to the five bundles of experience (*khandhas* – body, feeling-tone, perceptions, inclinations, and consciousness), or to the four focuses of awareness (*satipaṭṭhānas*), as the sum total of what constitutes us and what's going on. And what do we find when we look closely? *Just process* – arising and passing away. Nothing solid.

But not nothing either. The whole practice addresses the process of our *moral agency* – how we manifest in our several life-worlds as we cultivate what we care about. It challenges us to account for what we really do *care* about, for what drives our choices and directs our energies.

At the same time, the Buddha rejects the kind of disengaged 'knowledge' that Heidegger too rejects. The meditator is *always already* fully engaged, right there in the thick of it. Our authentic knowing (our consciousness) concerns what is happening right now. This knowing frees us from the static, habitual perceptions that enthral us. It sets us free.

Chapter 5

Martin Hägglund, secular faith and spiritual freedom

Heidegger's *Being and time*, the focus of the previous chapter, exercises a formative influence on my second western thinker who can help us fill out a secular retrieval and adaptation of the dharma: Martin Hägglund in his recent book, *This life: secular faith and spiritual freedom*. In what follows I'll glean those aspects of his thought that have implications for secular dharma practice. However, I want to preserve his overall argument intact, and so leave most of the specifically dharmic applications to the last section of this chapter.

Hägglund's main contribution consists largely in drawing out and grounding Heidegger's insights into what makes our lives matter. It thus enriches secular dharmic inquiry and practice, even though Hägglund himself doesn't identify with Buddhism in any way. In fact, he brackets conventional Buddhism with Christianity as manifestations of the 'religious faith' he rejects. These religions simply offer alternative ways to draw our attention away from what matters in our finite, time-bound lives (our 'being-towards-death' in Heidegger's term), he argues. Religious faith focuses instead on the prospect of salvation in an eternal (time*less*) realm beyond suffering. In this way he also indicates what we might think about abandoning in conventional Buddhist doctrine and practice.

Though he addresses his book to both secular and religious readers, he starts from the premise that we're all going to die at an unpredictable point in time, and that death is final. His main title, *This life,* refers to the only life we'll ever have on this premise, and so the one we must imbue with ultimate meaning. His book explores the implications of our essential finitude – our limited and uncertain lifespan, and our dependence on others. It does so in terms of a contrast between two pure models (or ideal types) of faith as such: religious faith and secular faith.

Religious faith

Religious faith denies the finality of death. According to it, this present earthly life is 'unsatisfactory', a fallen state of tribulation. If we fulfil the requirements our religion lays down, we will be redeemed from the torments of this life (including death as an absolute terminus) and dwell in eternal bliss – perhaps with an eternal god as guarantor, perhaps after several more earthbound lifetimes of spiritual practice. Hägglund doesn't join today's militant atheists in debunking this vision as scientifically implausible. Rather, he draws out its life-denying implications.

Religious faith places the agonies, losses and uncertainties of human life centre-stage. Its mission is to ameliorate them in our earthly lives, and after that to absolve us from them altogether. Amelioration typically takes the form of *renunciation*, a strategy first recommended by the ancient Greek stoics and some equally ancient Indian spiritualities, and then later doctrines right up to Spinoza's writings.

The path of renunciation requires us to condemn desire as such as a sign of lack, of spiritual impoverishment. For St Augustine, what we're lacking is God, and to immerse ourselves in the godhead is to overcome lack (p. 89). In conventional Buddhism desire comes across as a mental blight to be overcome through the development of insight, preferably while practising renunciation.

We can agree that we often indulge in unhelpful, and even destructive desires. Yet this general renunciant approach threatens to impoverish rather than ameliorate the lives we're actually living. Our most basic desires (for safety, food, drink and sex) underpin our very survival, while our more sophisticated, acculturated desires (for love, intimacy, sociality, knowledge, experience and self-expression, for instance) enrich our lives.[2]

The religious strategy here is to detach from – cease to care about – the relationships and things of this world, and instead dedicate heart and soul to an eternal god, presence, or promised blissful realm. Thus detached, we can reach for the analgesic that the stoics recommended under the rubric 'apathy' (*apatheia*), and that Buddhist monasticism offers as serenity based on detachment from all worldly cares. The religious game-plan for this life thus consists in leaving suffering behind, and achieving happiness understood simply as the absence of suffering – a foretaste of eternal post-mortem bliss.

Few if any human lives turn out to be an uninterrupted dance on roses, but we might question whether the avoidance of suffering deserves the dignity of constituting life's ultimate meaning. That doubt might lead us to pose the further question: what else matters apart from avoiding suffering, and might even take precedence over it?

We might also wonder why an eternal life of timeless bliss should appear so attractive to striving mortals like us. Our lives largely consist of love for our fellow mortals and projects that can fail, rising to challenges, overcoming difficulties, and events – all of which belong in the temporal dimension and so attract the Latin adjective *saecularis*. As we saw in the previous chapter, these phenomena constitute our very being in Heidegger's account, and would therefore be absent in an already-perfect, timeless realm. How would this sort of eternal life, devoid of all vitality, differ from being dead for such beings as we are?[3] (Indeed, Theravādin Buddhism spells out this equation: the ultimate goal is to exit the interminable round of life and death, and enter into 'extinction'.)

We'll return to these questions. For now we might count the cost of this religious game-plan. It takes the form of devaluing what accords us a sense of fulfilment and purpose, such as nurturing family and other love-based relationships, activism around social and environmental issues to create a safer and more just world, self-improvement, and following our curiosity about our inner and outer worlds. These are all forms of care which we lavish on other people and projects that are in themselves just as temporary and at-risk as we ourselves are. Otherwise we wouldn't care about them at all. It makes no sense to care for what is by definition already safe, eternal and self-fulfilled.

Of course many people engage in philanthropic work in the name of their religion. Most religions encourage kindness, generosity, compassion, and sometimes even social justice. But as Adam Phillips and Barbara Taylor show in their wonderful little book from 2009, *On kindness*, performing good works on religious recommendations, within a religious rewards system, introduces a transactional element into our motivation. Do we really care about these others we're helping, or are we merely accumulating credit points to be cashed in when we die? Is kindness then an end in itself, or a means to some other end?

There are many eloquent witnesses to the poor fit between religious faith and what really matters to us when it comes to the crunch. Hägglund dwells on the real agonies that overtook three outstanding Christian practitioners of religious faith: St Augustine, Martin Luther and CS Lewis. Each lost someone very close to them (a close friend, a daughter, and a wife respectively), was overwhelmed with grief, and reflected on the experience in an eloquent memoir or 'confession'.

In the next chapter we'll explore the way that grief strikes everyone who attains mature years; it's one of our most powerful and unpleasant emotions, yet one we have to work through, as this work deepens and seasons us. But Hägglund draws our attention to something else: all three of these religious figures reported how their intense grief was laced with guilt that they were mourning at all – giving in to 'cupidity' and becoming stuck in 'the glue of care', according to Augustine (quoted on pp. 74, 90) – instead of remaining firmly focused on God, the hereafter and the eternal.

Rather than modelling religious faith, they ended up exemplifying its opposite: secular faith. Indeed, Hägglund casts Augustine in the role of stalking horse as he develops his concept of secular faith.

Secular faith

For Hägglund secular faith represents an existential commitment – an expression of strong *fidelity* – to be wholeheartedly enacted, just like religious faith. Hence we should never confuse it with mere dismissal of religious revelations. He follows Kierkegaard in asserting that to embrace a faith of any sort is to transform our entire existence (p. 126). Practitioners of secular faith seek to intensify and extend *this life* as far as possible ('living on'), based on the conviction that this life, here and now, is worth living, and not to be devalued by hankering after an eternal life somewhere else and at another time. *Living on* trumps eternal life! It is 'secular' in the sense that we ourselves, everything we touch, and the events that make up our lives, all exist in time and are thus *saecularis*; we have no truck with entities and processes that supposedly transcend time.

Secular faith has three aspects: an existential commitment to sustaining fragile but significant relationships and projects; accepting uncertainty as a basic condition; and using the precariousness of every aspect of our lives as 'a *motivational force*' (p. 50). Because we ourselves and everything in our life-worlds are at risk, they are also *at stake*, and highly significant to us. In this way they command our care in themselves. 'The risk of loss is thus an essential part of the dynamic of secular faith,' Hägglund writes (p. 51).

Finitude and time are the core issues for secular faith, while care is its ethical underpinning. The days of our lives are limited but uncertain, and everyone and everything that we care about are bound to the same precarious, temporal dimension. Our very vitality depends on our finitude; death is the horizon towards which we're all working, and it must inform our choices and experiences in this life.

'Only someone who is finite can sense the miracle of being alive,' Hägglund writes (p. 106). When we come in close to death (at the funeral of a loved one, or in the presence of a corpse, perhaps) we might meet fear and love, terror and beauty – sublime, formative experiences (c.f. p. 119). So our mortality isn't a restriction – it's the mainspring of our secular passion in whose light 'every moment trembles on the verge of the past and the future' (p. 106). Mortality urges us to make the most of this life, sustaining our fidelity to it. '*Indifference is one of the seven deadly sins, actually the greatest of them all, because it is the only one that sins against life,*' he quotes one of his principal sources, the prominent novelist Karl Ove Knausgaard (p. 97).

This positive evaluation of finitude and mortality in no way gainsays the majesty of death itself – the tragic snuffing out of a unique life, its ceasing to exist in time.[4] As already noted, mourning our dead contributes vitally to our own development. (We'll return to this theme in the next chapter.) But it's also important to commemorate the dead – for their legacy in our own lives and life-worlds – as part of *their* living on.[5]

Seizing this life in time

Ecce distentio est vita mea! (See, my life is distended!), Augustine declares in his *Confessions* (quoted at p. 90). Hägglund creatively explores the concept of lived time as *distended* in ways that can shed light on the possibilities of insight (or 'mindfulness') meditation in dharma practice. The process of distention (Augustine's *distentio*) holds something together while also tending to stretch it and tear it apart. An overfull stomach illustrates the experience of distention, albeit in a negative way. But the experience doesn't have to be negative. If we simultaneously sift through our memories, pay careful attention to our present experience, and project into the future, then we can summon up a sense of life's fullness, while also acknowledging that time will eventually tear each of us apart. If we neglect our memories and fail to pay attention to our experiences in the present, then we commit the deadly sin of indifference and betray our secular faith.

We're not talking about clock and calendar time in this context, but experienced time. We experience time in our bodies, as 'embodied time' (*temps incorporé*) according to Marcel Proust, another of Hägglund's major sources (p. 112). With all our accumulating scars, healed fractures, internal wear and tear and ageing features, we carry our past with us into the present, inscribed in the body. Not forgetting that remarkable fleshy archive, the brain itself, that can not only record events, but help us re-live the feelings that accompanied them.

Hägglund ruminates at length on the two modern distenders of time already mentioned, Proust and Knausgaard. Like the much earlier Augustine – whose *Confessions* comprise thirteen volumes – both of the modern writers produced very long memoirs (*In search of lost time* and *My struggle*, in seven and six volumes respectively). But they produced them in the form of novels, in which the protagonist in each bears the author's given name. All three authors revive memories in minute and exorbitant detail on a mission to grasp the true meaning of their lives (although the redemptive meaning of Augustine's is a given from the start). In this way they *dilate* past time, increasing the distention of lived time as such. Proust influenced Knausgaard, but that didn't prevent the latter breaking the Proustian mould in a way crucial to Hägglund's argument.

Any experienced dharmic insight meditator would likely find Proust's and Knausgaard's narration of their memories familiar ground. Here we meet precise perceptions, minute details, and an indefatigable curiosity about the evanescent details in each event, feeling and experience. In dharmic terms they exemplify the second of the traditional seven factors of awakening – investigation-of-*dhammas* (phenomena) – even though they're delving into remembered phenomena rather than present ones.

Proust's search for lost time is precisely limited to time past. He retired into a reclusive existence, putting his life on hold, in order to retrieve the rich tapestry of his past life. Nostalgia becomes a refuge from the demands of the present (p. 109). For Knausgaard on the other hand, retrieval of the past was only part of the 'struggle' of his title – his struggle to own his own life, to understand its sources and its dynamics. So he splices his recollections into the ongoing life in which he's writing, with all its demands, embarrassments, distractions and conundrums. The past has no settled meaning; it can't speak for itself. It has to be refracted through the feelings, experiences, hopes and fears that constitute the present in order to contribute to the meaning of this life.

Again, an insight meditator would recognise this splicing of memory and present experience – it is part of the *sampajañña* (clear understanding) that accompanies meticulous recollection and awareness (*sati*). At intervals Knausgaard takes time out for lengthy musings about what all these patterns mean.

At the end of his distended work, Knausgaard signals mission accomplished. He has succeeded in his struggle to own his own life. But he's achieved no purification, redemption, or vacuous state of happiness beyond suffering. He wasn't looking for any of that. His life just continues, now with added clarity and commitment to it.

The most powerful insight he gains, after six volumes of relentless self-absorption, concerns the force of love in his life, and his utter dependence on those who set this life up for him, and who share this life with him now. He emerges as a prophet of *attachment*, poles apart from those of religious faith who advocate (but seldom achieve) detachment. Hägglund comments:

> The love that radiates here is the love of a life that is secular in Augustine's sense: bound by time, marked by history, dependent on generations that have come before and may come after. Throughout *My struggle* this temporal dimension is shown to hold the key to the passions of our lives. This distention of time marks every moment, but it can be stretched out in different ways and discloses the depths of who we are (p. 121).

Many an insight meditator has been waylaid by that self-same insight.

Spiritual freedom and responsibility

To exercise ownership over our life is to satisfy Heidegger's second criterion of authentic living (after constant awareness of death): freedom from *das Man* (the 'they' which imposes conventional expectations on us). In like fashion Hägglund identifies *spiritual freedom* as the value that secular faith enshrines, in contrast to the salvation that religious faith offers. Religious salvation holds out the prospect of freedom *from* finite life; secular faith and its spiritual freedom seek the liberation *of* finite life (pp. 208, 211). Spiritual freedom comes down to 'the ability to ask which imperatives to follow in light of our ends, as well as the ability to call into question, challenge, and transform our ends themselves' (p. 175). Religious faith specifies non-negotiable ends (and often means), foreclosing on this freedom, and thus the ethical responsibility that it underpins (p. 208).

Needless to say, spiritual freedom doesn't countenance amorality, nihilism or fecklessness, since they arise from the cardinal sin of indifference. Like any other freedom, spiritual freedom invokes responsibilities and relies on principles that potentiate and govern its exercise – all of which are normative in nature. As our everyday language makes clear, we *lead* our lives; we don't merely *live* them, and Hägglund has a deal to say about how that leadership (or moral agency) works (p. 188).

Each of us has a finite life span and a limited number of hours in the day in which to exercise our freedom of choice of ends and means. Usually each of us chooses a number of what he calls '*practical identities*': as a friend, a life partner, a parent, a productive worker, an active citizen, and so on. Each of these practical identities brings with it a standard of integrity against which we can fail or succeed.

But our limited time forces us to allocate it (and other scarce resources) to these practical identities, and in this way each of us shoulders an overriding responsibility to make the best sense of her/his life as a whole. This responsibility upholds our '*existential identity*' – in other words, our moral agency (pp. 188-9). This is not a static, fixed identity, but one that depends on unceasing questioning, adjustment to changing circumstances, and effort. This is the identity a good secular dharma practitioner upholds. Here we find ourselves in the heartland of secular *faith*, which demands our energetic, ongoing fidelity.

The multifaceted finitude we contend with, as we strive to maintain a coherent moral agency, generates a creative anxiety. 'My anxiety is not reducible to a psychological condition that can or should be overcome,' Hägglund notes (p. 192). 'Rather, anxiety is a condition of intelligibility for leading a free life and being passionately committed.' Heidegger makes much the same point in *Being and time.* 'Existential anxiety is a sign of our spiritual freedom,' Hägglund adds (p. 202).

Secular faith and secular dharma practice

To a large extent, secular dharma practitioners can read Hägglund's *This life* as a prompt to restore the Buddha's early teachings to their thrust before religious institutions laid claim to them and reworked them. An obvious example is the need to restore nirvana to its original meaning of an immediately available, transitory mind state free of greed, hatred and delusion, a meaning expressed in the first two chapters of this book. Later religification repurposed nirvana to stand for a timeless realm beyond suffering, one that Hägglund quite fairly brackets with the heavens of other religions.

That centrepiece of conventional Buddhism – suffering (*dukkha*) – calls for a little more work. In Part I we also saw how the work of Ñānavīra Thera and Stephen Batchelor restored the original meaning of 'the four' in the Buddha's first discourse to refer to *tasks* (embracing suffering; abandoning greed, hatred and delusion; registering the experience of their absence (nirvana); and cultivating an ethical way of life conducive to spiritual practice), and not to timeless *truths.* The discourse specifies what dukkha comprises – birth, sickness, ageing, death, separation from whom and what we love; being thrown together with whom and what we detest, frustration, and our psycho-physical vulnerability. No living person of mature years can avoid any of these exigencies, and there is no suggestion in the early teachings that we can 'go beyond' them short of physical death.

On the other hand, effective dharma practice can spare us, and those around us, a great deal of gratuitous suffering to the extent that we can – as we should – reduce the role of greed, hatred and delusion in our lives. Unfortunately, conventional Buddhism conflates both kinds of suffering and (in its distortion of the second task/truth) ascribes the whole lot to our benighted 'craving'. Unless one adopts a belief in rebirth and so denies the finality of death, this explanation makes no sense. Who can remember 'craving' to be born in the first place?

In many difficult times and places the prospect of a free pass from all suffering would have been (and would remain) hard to resist, even when presented as a long shot, as it is to lay practitioners of conventional Buddhism. However, today's western dharma practitioners might cast doubt on both the plausibility of the omnibus free pass, and the salience of suffering-avoidance in their practice. They might also seek to exempt the passionate desires that drive their lives forward from the 'craving' that should be abandoned as the root of all suffering. Even after correcting the interpretation of the early teachings, we might need to have the courage to adapt them to our current circumstances and de-emphasise the role of suffering-avoidance in our motivation to practise. We can place the emphasis instead on how we practise the dharma as our guide to the exercise of spiritual freedom in our quest for full human flourishing.

Hägglund's discussion of spiritual freedom should greatly reinforce that motivation and effort. It compellingly presents the development and rewards of moral agency that fit well with the dharma. Like the Buddha, Hägglund makes *care* the driver of his ethical thought. His working terms based on 'identity' will probably find disfavour among those Buddhists who believe that the Buddha denied the existence of the self, for instance by misinterpreting *anattā* (Pali for the meditative experience not-self, of not being a fixed entity) as referring to a metaphysical claim that the self does not exist. In fact, an implicit sense of selfhood as moral agency runs throughout the teachings, and occasionally becomes explicit, as in the oft-repeated verse 80 of the *Dhammapada:*

> Just as a farmer irrigates his field,
> just as a fletcher fashions an arrow,
> just as a carpenter shapes a piece of wood,
> so the sage tames the self.

Hägglund's presentation of the free spiritual practitioner in terms of practical and existential identities, and of the need for coherence in and fidelity to this life, crystallises this crucial aspect of dharma practice.

His discussion of the distention (or dilation) of embodied time through meticulous remembering of the past and acute awareness of present experience throws a new light on insight meditation and its contribution to human flourishing. The instructions for *vipassanā* meditation – the monastic version of the practice, often still taught under monastic tutelage – draw our attention to the shifting, contingent nature of our experience when observed in its fine grain. But we're often told, as well, what to make of this insubstantial pageant: our worldly experience is 'unsatisfactory' frippery, to be laid aside, to be *detached from*. We're also discouraged from connecting the dots between past and present, from seeing our experience in narrative form beyond immediate links of cause and effect.

Following Knausgaard, Hägglund shows how fine-grained attention to our memories and our present experience can take us off in the opposite direction, deepening our appreciation of – and intelligent commitment to – those *attachments* that imbue our lives with substance and meaning. Perhaps this effect partly explains the efficacy of mindfulness meditation in its psychotherapeutic applications. Certainly for the secular insight meditator in the Buddha's tradition, Hägglund's presentation is both suggestive and bracing.

This chapter has discussed only the first major part of Hägglund's *This life*. His insights and ethic of care have compelling ramifications in our social and political lives as well, ones which he goes on to spell out in his book. I will return to them in chapter 16.

Chapter 6

Freud, dukkha and flourishing

Sigmund Freud sheds light on crucial and often overwhelming experiences we all have as mature individuals: loss, grief and mourning. These experiences take us to the Buddha's very own starting point – *dukkha* (suffering, dissatisfaction, anguish, frustration, stress). It's right there, centre-stage, in the Buddha's first discourse, which laid the foundations for his teachings from then on. So we need to clarify where dukkha fits into that teaching.

As we saw in Part I, orthodox Buddhism extrapolates its doctrine of the four noble truths from the first discourse: life is suffering (*dukkha*); craving is the cause of suffering; suffering can be overcome; and: the eightfold path leads to the end of suffering. Since the early 1960s some dharma practitioners have refuted this doctrine on four grounds: it doesn't square with what the discourse actually says, especially in its original form; the Buddha taught that life also consists of joy and the opportunity to awaken – not just suffering; it doesn't make sense to say that 'craving' is the cause of all suffering; the Buddha repeatedly rejected all metaphysical truth claims, and would not have made such claims the basis of his teaching.

A more naturalistic interpretation of the Buddha's first discourse renders the supposed four noble truths as four central *tasks* for a spiritual practitioner: embrace and fully understand suffering; on that basis let go of our habitual reactions to our difficult experiences; identify and savour the peace, spaciousness and lucidity we experience when we do let go of all our reactivity (however momentarily); and: let that experience propel us onto a path (a way of life) that builds on the wisdom that our practice of our central tasks generates.[6]

What is dukkha and how does it arise?

In that critical first discourse, the Buddha actually lists the elements of what he means by dukkha: birth, ageing, sickness, death, being separated from whom and what we love, being thrown together with whom and what we detest; not getting what we want, and our general psycho-physical vulnerability. (You might enjoy the challenge of discovering an annoyance that falls outside this list!)

This list suggests two things to us. Firstly, no human being who attains maturity can escape any one of the items on it. Secondly, the whole lot point back to our ever-present experience of (and insight into) *impermanence* – a major dharmic theme. As Shakespeare put it, 'We are such stuff as dreams are made on; and our little life is rounded with a sleep.'[7]

Or, as scientifically-minded souls point out: we're all subject to the law of entropy over time. 'Things fall apart,' as the Buddha noted in his last recorded sentence. And as Delmore Schwartz sums up the consequence in his poem 'Calmly we walk through this April's day':

Time is the school in which we learn,
Time is the fire in which we burn.

So dukkha stands for *inescapable* aspects of the human condition, whether we indulge in 'craving' or not.

Our habitual responses (probably based on evolutionary

factors) to dukkha moments are craving, aversion, and delusion – the three 'poisons' identified in the dharma. Major forms of delusion are the denial, suppression, and misunderstanding of the experience of suffering (for instance, by blaming and complaining). These evasions make matters worse – often far worse. We indulge them when we fail to embrace and fully understand the primary difficulties that life inevitably throws up for us.

A lot of the time we can absorb experiences of dukkha with a modicum of honesty, maturity, insight, humour and self-compassion, and emerge from them as wiser human beings. But lurking in the Buddha's list of dukkha elements is a real biggie: loss of someone or something very important to us. Usually this will be someone close to us – a life-partner, a parent, a child or a best friend. But it could also be something like a homeland, a culture and mother tongue, or an ideal.[8] Such losses, like serious trauma, demand heavy work to reinstate our sense of who we are.

Mourning and melancholia

Freud called this 'the unpleasant work' of mourning, in his still influential 1917 essay on the subject, 'Mourning and melancholia'.[9] Its basic theme is that we need to undertake this work as a serious response to a personally significant loss, if we're to emerge from it once more able to flourish. This psychoanalytic insight converges with the Buddha's first *task* – embracing and fully knowing dukkha.

If we shirk this work, Freud suggests, we condemn ourselves to a sort of half-life, melancholia. Instead of mourning the dead, we join them. In his time, cultural awareness of the importance of mourning was imprinted in everyday culture. Rituals and social customs (such as wearing black clothing or armbands) supported a bereaved person as s/he entered into a period of profound sadness, even controlled madness – certainly exceptional fragility.[10]

Today we have lost that social knowledge of the importance

of mourning, and how to undertake it and support others through it. Which is why so many of us ignore, neglect and trivialise mourning. Willy nilly we find ourselves refusing to mourn. Freud has a message for us in this predicament, too.

Mourning and flourishing

Much less visited among his collected works is a three-page memoir that Freud called 'On transience' – a title that should entice Buddhist readers. It concerns a hike he took in the Dolomites (the Italian alps) in August 1914:

> Not long ago I went on a summer walk through a smiling countryside in the company of a taciturn friend and of a young but already famous poet. The poet admired the beauty of the scene around us but felt no joy in it. He was disturbed by the thought that all this beauty was fated to extinction, that it would vanish when winter came, like all human beauty and all the beauty and splendour that people have created or may create. All that he would otherwise have loved and admired seemed to him to be shorn of its worth by the transience which was its doom...[But] it was incomprehensible, I declared, that the thought of the transience of beauty should interfere with our joy in it.[11]

The 'taciturn friend' has the same problem as the poet – which Freud diagnoses as a *refusal to mourn*. Or, in our terms, this is the refusal to perform the Buddha's first task: embracing and fully understanding suffering. And, of course, a vain refusal to live with impermanence (Freud's 'transience').

Where does such refusal lead? For Freud this fear of mourning leads to 'a permanent renunciation' which the poet and taciturn friend in the story exemplify – a saying 'no' to life that amounts to a self-impoverishment, because it's precisely change that brings us the abundance and riches of a well-lived life, including everyone and everything we love.[12]

So this permanent renunciation leaves no room for the joy and the opportunity to awaken that the Buddha also insisted were our birthright in the land of the living, and that underpin our flourishing as human beings. We cannot flourish as a human being, Freud concludes, unless we're prepared to mourn. If we do take on this 'work', we deepen as mature individuals; we're able to commit and love again, to live more fully when we've done it. But if we refuse this work, we can end up in a state of emotional death called melancholia.

Two life strategies in the face of impermanence

Western popular culture today demands that we have fun all the time. We used to have rituals and conventions for mourning, ones that respected an individual's need to do this work, which could take months or years, and to receive the community's acknowledgement and support for it. But these conventions (and the wisdom in them) have largely disappeared. Sad feelings are defined as a problem, and mourning is seen as some sort of pathology. We're now advised to take anti-depressants or see a therapist, or both, if we're feeling sad. No matter what the cause. These resources will allow us to 'get over it', 'find closure', and 'move on'.

This unhelpful attitude – a form of Freud's 'refusal to mourn' – has a good deal in common with the mistaken interpretation of the Buddha's teaching about 'detachment'. Both advise us to skip the hard bits in our human existence. But in that way they make us emotionally inadequate and stunt our development in the name of 'mental health' or spiritual 'detachment'. They try to persuade us to duck the challenge of impermanence in our lives.

The Buddha's (and Freud's) strategy goes off in the opposite direction: embrace our rich human life with all its deep emotional connections, and learn to ride the tiger of impermanence.

Chapter 7

Peter Watson

Mindfulness meditation isn't a technical skill that can be learned or practised in emotional downtime. Rather, it depends on our caring. While one of my early teachers was teaching a group of us mindfulness of breathing meditation, she gave the instruction, 'follow your breath as you would follow the breath of your own newborn baby!'

If you've ever given birth to another human being, or been present and participated in the birth of your own child, you might feel the power of this instruction. The child's first breaths are so fragile, and so momentous. A new human being has just arrived, one composed of your own flesh and blood; your life has suddenly been enriched and drastically changed. Can we carry that intensified care-full attention over to aspects of our lives we usually dismiss as too ordinary to even notice?

As we saw in Part I, the Buddha so prioritised care that he made it the centrepiece of his last words – final advice to his followers gathered round his deathbed: *Things fall apart: tread the path with care.* And here's the Buddha at his most drastic – in the *Dhammapada* – on the importance of care:

> Care is the path to the deathless;
> Carelessness is the path to death.
> The caring do not die;
> The uncaring are as already dead.

Here, care is of ultimate existential importance.

In this verse 'death' refers to a living death – being in the thrall of Māra, the personification of spiritual death, purveyor of reactivity in the form of greed, hatred and delusion. Reactivity switches off our engagement with life, our responsiveness and vitality. By cultivating care we avoid that fate. But if we become careless or uncaring by being habitually jaded, indifferent, cynical, and insensitive, we're on our way into a degraded life, a half-life.

In sum, the dharma is a path of care, and this makes it an ethical path that marshals and focuses our senses (and sensi*tivities*), our emotions and our intelligence into our transformative endeavour to live a more authentic, meaningful and dignified human life.

The come-and-see (*ehipasiko*) dharma asks us to deepen, to live and practise more *intensely*. When Māra tried to tempt the Buddha to put his feet up and take it easy in his old age, the Buddha retorted that we should live and practise as if our hair were on fire. Now *there's* an intense experience!

Intensity as a modern virtue

Many modern thinkers agree with the Buddha here, and Peter Watson brings them together in his 2014 book, *The age of atheists: how we have sought to live since the death of God*. The title calls for a spot of unravelling. In 1881 Friedrich Nietzsche announced that God is dead. This death notice has reverberated in western thought down to our own time. Nietzsche wasn't interested in 'the God question' (whether or not such an entity exists), but rather was making an observation that leading western thinkers no longer premised their work on his (or her) existence and enforceable demands. Instead of deriving our first principles about how to live from holy texts, we now have to work them out for ourselves. We have to take on the responsibility to figure out what really matters. We've graduated from the child restraint in the car to the driver's seat.

The 'atheists' in Watson's title aren't co-religionists of to-day's militant atheists; they're merely people who've explored first principles to live by in the absence of God. Together they've produced what's often referred to as 'the death of God literature' – hence Watson's subtitle. Instead of starting with metaphysical revelations in holy texts, they've started from the only material available to them: sensuous human experience in this lived world of ours. Experience displaces fussing about other worlds, their demands, and how to attain them. The novelist Henry James dismissed transcendental ideas as 'shared fictions'. To reach down into our own experience, we need to abandon these metaphysical distractions. As we've already seen, the Buddha gave the same advice.

In our western culture, unfortunately, Watson's post-metaphysical thinkers face stiff competition from false gods which have sprung up to replace the deceased one and associated beliefs. Consumerism, money-love, affluence theologies, and other forms of 'selfing' typify these false gods. They encourage *complacency, triviality and protective shallowness*, Watson suggests. There's little caring or vibrancy going on in those mental spaces!

The thinkers that Watson glosses reject these gods too. By their separate paths and in their different idiom, they come to the same conclusion as André Malraux: the meaning of life 'must lie in its intensity'.[13]

The Buddha's most detailed advice on how to intensify our experience of our being-there and being-in-the-world (to use Martin Heidegger's expressions) is contained in the *Satipaṭṭhāna sutta*, the canonical source of insight meditation. The sutta contains no technical instructions, requires the development of no technical proficiency. It's free of esotericism and the promise of metaphysical revelations. (There are none to be had.) What we need to understand will arise out of our own care-fully observed experience, and the practice will bring us to understand it *viscerally*.

The sutta culminates in the contemplation of the four tasks. But they're in fact present at all stages in dharma practice. They require us to fully embrace the inevitable difficulties of the human condition, including our finitude; to let go of our instinctive and habitual evasions of those difficulties through craving, aversion and delusion; to awaken to moments of profound stillness that accompany their temporary absence; and cultivate a multifaceted way of life that deepens our ethical and spiritual development.[14]

One of the thinkers that Peter Watson gathers into his fold is precisely Martin Heidegger, whom we met in chapter 4. He also identified care (*Sorge*) as the mainspring of an authentic human life, one intensely lived. Like the Buddha, Heidegger also introduced the tempering value of letting-go (*Gelassenheit*).

To live intensely must never translate into wilfulness – into our turning into meddling control freaks as we cultivate receptivity. Were we to fall into that trap, we'd be blocking the sensitive exploration of our experience. Thus Heidegger extols calm, composure, detachment, release – letting things be.[15] This principle comes close to the Buddha's *upekkha* (equanimity), one of the four vital 'immeasurable' emotional tones of the awakening mind.

This is what it means, as well, to live a life of integrity, to live *authentically*, in full acknowledgement of our finitude, and with the determination to steer our own course in the face of conventional expectations. No small task!

We need to know about the four great tasks, and it's a great advantage to know the *Satipaṭṭhāna sutta* inside out. But what we need as much as anything else is to sustain the urgency and intensity of our practice.

We westerners aren't used to working in a goalless way. We want to achieve goals, cross finishing lines, receive the commemorative silverware, maybe even a a certificate of full enlightenment. Otherwise we tend to lose interest, and turn to something that offers instant and more palpable gratification.

The greater blessing we can give ourselves is what Zen practitioners call 'beginner's mind'. It's the royal road to living intensely. If our meditative and life experience isn't fresh and vivid, then maybe we're not going deep enough, not sloughing off dulling habits of mind. Are we on automatic pilot? Are we treating our practice as routine, even a hobby, at worst a chore, and something apart from our 'real' lives?

We need to deliberately unlock our capacity for care, curiosity, delight and amazement. We can do this by keeping our sources of inspiration close at hand. And let some of them be nature, poetry, art, and our sangha. Our practice communities are palpable manifestations of care. Meditation, and dharma practice in general, are communal undertakings. In our individualistic culture it's easy to lose sight of this basic fact.

But above all, we need to come back to the big picture that our own culture makes available to us – the one Watson extols – with its promptings to lead this one precious life in a spirit of urgency, intensity and authenticity, as well as letting-go.

Notes

1   Heidegger [1927] 2008.

2   I broached this theme in chapter 2, in the context of Rorty's (1991: 154) two competing models of spiritual life – self-purification versus self-enlargement.

3   As we saw in chapter 1, Martha Nussbaum (1990: 379) makes this point in her critique of the 'external transcendence' that religious faith offers.

4   Of all the euphemisms for dying that I've come across, the only one that appeals is the Swedish *att gå ur tiden*: literally, 'to go out of time'.

5   As Thomas Laqueur (2015) shows, the dead still have 'work' to do, in undergirding the cohesion of the living.

6   See Ñāṇavīra Thera, 2001 Vol II: 106–7; Batchelor 2015: ch. 3.

7   *The tempest*, IV/1.

8   George Prochnik (2015) presents a moving example of this grief. See also Martin Hägglund's examples in the previous chapter. Joyce Kornblatt's (2020) compelling novel, *Mother tongue*, plumbs this kind of suffering from a dharmic perspective.

9   Strachey and Freud 1957: 243–304.

10 Joan Didion (2007 and 2011) has given us two exceptional retrievals of this process of mourning. Darian Leader (2009) underlines its enduring importance.

11 Strachey & Freud 1957: 305. This memoir comes immediately after 'Mourning and melancholia' in the standard edition of Freud's collected works.

12 As we've seen in the previous chapter, Martin Hägglund (2020: ch. 1) makes much of this theme in his discussion of 'secular faith'

13 Quoted in Watson 2014: 340.

14 C.f. Batchelor 2015: ch. 3.

15 C.f Inwood 1999: 117.

Part III

The inner life

Chapter 8

Renewing the practice from first principles

The four tasks and the eightfold path (the fourth of the tasks) discussed in chapters 1 and 2 constitute the kernel of the Buddha's teaching. They form a feedback loop. The tradition helpfully regroups the eight folds of the path under three heads of practice ('the three great trainings') of ethics, meditation and wisdom. How can we adapt and use them today? Let's approach the question historically, as secularity indicates we should.

Community and ethics at the dawn of the tradition

According to the tradition, the Buddha died aged 80 around 400 BCE. He'd been teaching for 45 years and had a large following in what is now northeastern India. This following comprised women and men, renunciants and householders, from all walks of life. He himself had been born and raised in the small Sakiyan oligarchical republic, and in guiding his scattered small renunciant communities he followed what we'd recognise today as civic-republican principles.

That is to say, all members were full participants in independent, ideally harmonious communities – 'flat organisations' we might call them in today's managementese. They had no use for leaders. They owned nothing and relied on the goodwill of small-time monarchs, other notables, and ordinary folk for protection and sustenance. Apart from that, they were quite feral, in particular following the Buddha's lead in not respecting the reigning caste and gender systems.

Over time, the Buddha had to deal with the usual hassles of communal life. Again in an ad hoc way, he developed rules for his renunciant communities in order to harmonise and simplify them, rules that eventually comprised the *Vinaya*. For his followers in general, though, he simplified his ethical stance down to five precepts which, expressed in positive form, assert the values of universal friendliness, generosity, contentment, honesty and mental clarity.

Note that the precepts indeed constituted an *ethic* – an assertion of fundamental values – as opposed to a *morality* (i.e., a rule book). An ethic challenges our self-responsibility, intelligence and sensitivity; it calls on us to take responsibility as moral agents each time we have to make an ethically significant decision. We can't get by as moral agents simply by following the rules – we have to consider the consequences of our decisions as best we can. What an ethic demands of us will vary according to our socioeconomic, political and cultural context. Hold that thought.

Except during the rainy season, the Buddha was constantly on the move, visiting these communities, answering their questions and addressing their internal difficulties. This pattern suited the Buddha's teaching practice: turn up on the outskirts of a town, have his renunciant followers or the townsfolk toss him questions and real-world conundrums, and spontaneously answering them.

He explained the principles of meditation in some detail, but never reduced them to how-to technical instructions. He gave no planned sermons, no scheduled lectures, used no PowerPoint presentations, just off-the-cuff, highly situational *performance pieces*. In today's euphemism, these conversations were 'frank and fearless' on both sides. No one learned anything by grovelling deferentially. Such are the *suttas* we inherit, the discourses of the Buddha in the Pali canon.

Institutional imperatives and meditation

In the centuries following his death, however, all this changed. Buddhism became organised as a religion, and took on the trappings of a religion-like-any-other. Semi-feral renunciants morphed into monastics organised into large, regimented units structured around hierarchies. The Buddha's ad hoc, off-the-cuff teachings were codified into orthodox translations and commentaries.

Impatient with the one-off, contextual nature of the suttas, some brave monastics decided to distil them into what they called – not without hubris – 'the higher teaching', the seamless *Abhidhamma*. It's full of metaphysical truth-claims, and among other things became the basis of technique-heavy *vipassanā* meditation developed above all in Burmese and Thai monasteries. (Along with Zen, this form of meditation achieved prominence among western adherents under Buddhist-modernist auspices in the latter 20th century.)

In accounting for this development and its knock-on effects in the Buddhist world today, the far-reaching effects of *institutionalisation* are often missed. Inevitably, power relations become the dominant issue, both inside a large institution and between it and its host society.

Especially in pre-modern times, large-scale organised religions of all stripes wielded enormous social and cultural power, and their hierarchs tended to align themselves with other power-holders – temporal rulers and socio-economic elites. The religious hierarchs legitimated rulers and social elites by promoting social integration on the basis of the elites' conservative patriarchal values, including the subordination and marginalisation of women. The hierarchs deflected criticism of – and challenge to – the powers that be by propagating submissiveness among the laity as a spiritual virtue.

To sustain their external and internal power, Buddhist monastic hierarchs had to train a disciplined cadre of subordinate monks. Enforcement of the monastic rule and a particular approach to teaching meditation served this purpose. The need to exercise authority and train a cadre, rather than support individuals' spiritual quests, changed the way that meditation was taught. It became highly technical, *formulaic*, based on the metaphysics of the *Abhidhamma*. Celibate males living regimented, institutionalised lives were drilled in standardised meditation techniques to produce standardised experiences. Non-standard experiences were thus deemed to be 'not meditation' and frowned upon.

The standardised experiences, duly 'reported' to one's teacher, could in turn be certified at prescribed checkpoints to facilitate an orderly promotion process based on 'spiritual attainment'. Spiritual progress came down to compliance with the template.

Retrieving non-formulaic meditation

When we look at the account of the Buddha's own main teaching on meditation, the *Satipaṭṭhāna sutta* (the discourse on the four focuses of awareness), unsurprisingly we find no such agenda. Consistent with the focus of the four tasks on the human condition, the leitmotiv of the Buddha's teaching is human *experience* in all its variety and complexity.

Meditation is for sharpening our senses to delve more deeply into our individual direct experience of being-in-the-world, and thereby coming to understand its cause-and-effect dynamics, and so by degrees coming to embrace and negotiate it more skilfully. As we've all seen, surely, the flow of human experience is unpredictable, complex and multilayered.

So as not to lose the plot as we try to become aware of all this complexity, the Buddha asks us to account for our direct experience in four areas – roughly: physical; feeling-tone; emotional;

and cognitive. If our attention tends to narrow into one of these areas, we have an instruction to check out what is happening in the other three as well, so we enter into our experience more fully and see the whole pattern.

Naturally, meditative approaches that work to formulas, and ask us to shun large slabs of our experience as 'not meditation', are false friends. When we sit down with the intention of meditating, all experience from that point until the end of the session is meditative experience.[1] We don't need a technique to cull and trim our meditative experience.

Conclusion

Let's return to the three great trainings. What are they asking of us today, as relatively well-off, well-educated individuals – citizens of affluent and fairly stable democracies, thus leading highly unusual, privileged lives compared to how most humans live and have lived?

Ethics

Mere compliance with a set of rules doesn't even scratch the surface of our ethical responsibilities. We practitioners have signed up to an ethic of universal friendliness to all sentient life, generosity, contentment, honesty, and lucidity. It challenges us in the unique and immediate circumstances of our individual lives, in how we treat those around us, those we meet on the daily round, what we buy (having checked out its source) and how we vote and participate in civic life (given the contribution our elected representatives could be making to human and non-human ill- or well-being).

As I will argue in Part V of this book, dharmic ethics requires us to confront the two crises that are overwhelming life on earth right now – the climate emergency, and the ballooning inequalities and social exclusions on every level of collective existence, from the global to the local. It isn't ethical to turn our backs on these crises, or to pretend that we're helping by simply honing our meditation practice.

In the Buddha's time, political life and institutions barely existed and had negligible impact on well-being. Back then the calamities that afflicted people were diseases (almost all curable now), famine, natural disasters, and violence. There were no political remedies for these calamities. But now organisational decisions (government and corporate) deeply affect all our lives – in promoting global warming, environmental degradation, mass death from preventable diseases, malnutrition, growing relative deprivation within and between countries, warfare and genocide, and the systemic maltreatment of other species.

The Buddhist ethic carries major implications for how we tackle or duck our civic responsibilities to minimise suffering and promote human flourishing.

Meditation

As we saw above, a great deal of what passes for Buddhist meditation today was originally designed to train and regiment celibate men living in total institutions. Hence its formulaic nature, and its claim to be 'authoritative' and 'the one true way'. But today hardly any of us are celibate men, and we're living highly complex, individuated lives. On the basis of the Buddha's own teaching on meditation, we need to forge meditation practices that directly tackle the four tasks in the first teaching, that is, ones that embrace the whole of the human condition and work with it. We need to master the principles of meditation and learn to manage our own practices intelligently.

Wisdom

In Buddhism this, too, is a *practice*, but a derivative one. Carefully observing the outcomes of our ethically significant actions teaches us invaluable life skills. As does a gentle, exploratory receptiveness towards our unfettered meditation experience. Giving practical effect to what we learn in these two ways goes to the core of what it means to *practise* wisdom.

Chapter 9

Secular insight practice and everyday awakening

In recent times I've led a study of the *Satipaṭṭhāna sutta* (the Buddha's discourse on the focuses of awareness), as translated and expounded by Anālayo[2] for three lay insight-meditation sanghas in Sydney. In each case the study took 18 sessions, even though the sutta itself is only 10 pages long.

It deserves this lavish attention, given that it's the foundational teaching for insight meditation. In theory, it's also the basis of *vipassanā* meditation, although later commentaries and monastic adaptations loom larger for it in practice. Putting time and effort into plumbing the sutta gets us out of the passive, even consumerist approach we often bring to our spiritual choices. Through detailed study we get to own our meditation practice in an active sense. Among lay practitioners, the sutta is a bit like the Bible, Marcel Proust's *In search of lost time*, and James Joyce's *Ulysses*: greatly revered, their titles aired in countless contexts and conversations, but seldom actually read.

Many years ago I attended a talk on insight meditation by a Theravādin monk – an ethnic Australian one who was 'a bit of a character', as we say. There he sat cross-legged in his robes, his hair and eyebrows duly shaven off, and declared: 'I am not a Buddhist. No other labels fit me either. I'm just someone who studies and practises the *Satipaṭṭhāna sutta.*'

I had some sympathy with this position. But the sutta condenses and alludes to essential points of dharma, including most of the important classical lists – to which it adds three more, starting with the four focuses of awareness themselves, which I'll come to in a moment. So if one's life revolves around this sutta, as this monk said that his did, then you're certainly in an intimate relationship with the Buddhadharma!

Assuming the Buddha delivered this teaching in one session, then he did so late in his career. It draws on his long experience as a practitioner and a teacher. It condenses his teaching, and operationalises it for meditative purposes. Maybe, just like the monk in question, he wasn't a Buddhist either – that label was only invented two centuries ago, after all. Great innovators commonly find themselves having to disown the debased orthodoxy that their followers often distil from their ideas. Karl Marx explicitly said that he wasn't a Marxist, for instance.

A peep inside the sutta

The sutta in fact yields up three new lists and intertwines them. The most important and best-known of them sets out the four focuses of awareness (*satipaṭṭhāna*)

- experiences of the body (drawing on our crucial nature as *embodied* beings);
- feeling tones that arise with each experience of sense-contact;
- mind-states (moods and emotions); and finally
- *dhammas* (phenomena, cognitive contents of mind).

It's under the rubric of this fourth focus of awareness that the Buddha condenses his central teachings, from the five hindrances to the fourfold task (aka 'the four noble truths'). In general, the sutta offers us a choice of which of these focuses (and sub-focuses) to home in on in a sit or part of a sit, or to be open to all four at once. And the advice isn't limited to formal meditation – it's something we can take out into our everyday lives.

The first of the less well-known lists in the sutta is that of the four mental qualities we need to cultivate and bring to our awareness practice, on and off the cushion:

- diligence (*ātāpī*),
- clearly knowing (*sampajāna*),
- freedom from worldly desires and discontent, and above all
- our old friend *sati* (recollection and awareness: perhaps 'recollective awareness' – popularly known as mindfulness).

These mental qualities strengthen as we gain traction in the practice.

The third new list comes in the recurring 'refrains' after each focus of awareness is introduced. Here the sutta gives prominence to:

- the choice between contemplating experience either internally, or externally, or both internally and externally; or
- observing the rising and passing away (i.e., impermanence) of the elements of experience; or
- simply noting the existence of the area of experience in question, so as to facilitate 'bare knowledge' and 'continuous attention'.

Choice and creativity in insight meditation

In sum, the sutta offers us a lot of choice about where to take our practice at any particular time. The range of choices is greatly increased by the multiple exercises grouped under each of the four focuses. The emphasis on *choice* in the process of meditation (in the complete absence of formulaic instructions) might lead us to the sense that deliberate and creative process goes to the heart of the practice, which is designed for autonomous practitioners who practise 'independent of others'.

So the sutta is *not* providing us with a strip map for a journey from A to B along a single well-trodden track. Rather, it's providing a detailed concept map of a whole inner topography that we can explore along myriad alternative routes. We can follow our noses, or we can prioritise visiting certain features over others.

The map is there to help us to orient ourselves in our complex inner world, and make the best choices in our effort to practise the ancient trans-cultural wisdom of 'know thyself'. Put another way: the sutta allows us to *parse* our experience, so as to see how it works.

Pragmatism, and not metaphysics, drives the cartography. It and the choice of features on the map are *useful* for navigation purposes, rather than pointing to some sort of ultimate reality. That emphasis on usefulness colours the choice of the four focuses themselves – they don't point to some sort of absolute realities either. They serve a purpose, rather than offer revelations.

We don't know to what extent the sutta was edited and tampered with after the Buddha's death – during the 400 years or so when the Pali canon was still in a fluid state, and most of that time a purely oral tradition. But we can note that the sutta – as it stands – implicitly proposes *two divergent agendas*:

* the open-ended exploration of (and deepening into) our subjective experience on the one hand, and on the other
* the achievement of some sort of end-state 'realisation'/'final knowledge' understood as salvation or liberation.

If we were to seize on this second agenda, then we'd reduce the great map that the sutta unfurls to a GPS taking us to a palpable finishing line. We'd be using it in a goal-directed way.

I want to go further into this problem in the next chapter, when we look at how we can assert the first agenda (with its emphasis on an ethics-based process and awareness) over the second (with its goal-orientation towards salvation).

Two divergent paths of practice

We need to clarify our choice of where we want our spiritual lives to go, before we figure out how to apply the sutta. In the second chapter I mentioned the pragmatist philosopher Richard Rorty's two alternative models of spiritual development, and I'll expand on them in the present context.

In the Theravāda, one who has reached the finishing line and attained 'final knowledge' is called an *arahant*. Anālayo's presentation exemplifies this school when he describes the arahant in terms of *purity*. It's a big word, and a big ideal in his tradition, whose defining commentary is precisely called *The path of purification* (*Visuddhimagga*).

In Richard Rorty's terms, 'purity' evokes a sharp divergence in models of human development (and thus of spiritual practice), between *self-purification* and *self-enlargement* (which in this context has nothing to do with narcissism!) He explains the contrast like this:

The desire to purify oneself is the desire to slim down, to peel away everything that is accidental, to will one thing, to intensify, to become a more transparent being. [By contrast] the desire to enlarge oneself is the desire to embrace more and more possibilities, to be constantly learning, to give oneself over entirely to curiosity, to end by having envisaged all the possibilities of the past and of the future.[3]

To pursue purity requires belief in an enduring inner self or soul that can be 'purified' – liberated from taints, defilements and encumbrances – in order to attain a static and standardised conception of 'enlightenment', for instance. Whereas to pursue self-enlargement would incline us to see ourselves as works-in-progress unto death, ones with no essential inner core to work back to, and no one-size-fits-all spiritual terminus to work towards.

This latter model of spiritual development resonates with Heidegger's 'being-in-the-world' and Hägglund's idea of maintaining an 'existential identity' throughout one's lifetime, which we visited in chapters 4 and 5 respectively. The self-enlargement model leaves no room for a finishing line.

In popular philosophical parlance, one can view oneself as an artichoke which has a core underneath enfolding leaves, or as an onion which consists *only* of its enfolding leaves. These self-concepts imply contrasting spiritual projects.

Purity invokes a notion of perfection. But as products of a successful evolutionary process in a dangerous world, we humans simply aren't 'perfect'. The evolutionary factors of greed, hatred and delusion have made us the dominant species and remain intractably in our DNA, ready to surface at any careless moment.

Perfectionism, which can find expression in both religious and secular terms, in fact constitutes one of humanity's great frailties. It's a form of grandiosity that seeks an *exit* from the human condition, not an *exploration and enrichment* of it.

Were we actually to attain purity or perfection, we would cease to be human. And indeed, the models of purity and perfection on offer – from arahants to the saints and martyrs of other traditions – are precisely non-human, usually post- or super-human. They've transcended the human condition – that which the Buddha in his first discourse enjoins us to embrace! The Buddha himself certainly wasn't perfect: Māra (representing his basic human drives) kept trying to trip him up right to the end.

So maybe the practice of the sutta is more about becoming a deeper, more ethical and sensitive human being, than about ceasing to be human altogether. We can use its detailed mapping of our humanity for this kind of exploration, not as an aid to finding the quickest exit from it. The realisation and awakening it refers to is available right here in the human realm.

Chapter 10
From goal-orientation to honouring process

In the previous chapter we saw how the *Satipaṭṭhāna sutta* invites us to deepen into our immediate experience of being human in this world – to awaken all our senses so as to touch its richer and finer texture, to sharpen our intuitive intelligence in coming to grips with the way causation (dependent arising, or 'conditionality') works in our lives, and to gradually transform our way of being in the world accordingly.

This way of approaching insight practice seems to stay closer to the text than the conventional one, of seeing insight meditation (and dharma practice in general) as a GPS leading as directly as possible to the exit from the human condition itself. As we've seen earlier, dharma practice informs the fourfold task of embracing the human condition (especially its difficult aspects), letting go of reactivity when those difficult moments catch up with us, realising the peace and wisdom we experience in the absence of reactivity, and cultivating a multifaceted way of life ('path') that leads us to full human flourishing through this practice. In case we ever miss this point, the very last exercise that the Buddha suggests in the *Satipaṭṭhāna sutta* is precisely the contemplation of these four tasks.

The conventional Buddhist approach leads through self-purification to some post-human transcendence, salvation or redemption. So it is *goal-oriented.* It also imposes a standardising template on how each of us will manifest when we've trodden the path of purification, without regard to our unique preconditions, life experiences, and conditioning. If we take the conventional road to becoming exalted beings, and achieved 'the goal', we'd be stripped of our pasts and our individuality.

Three levels of practice

If we receive the sutta and the practice in the way I'm suggesting, however, we abandon goal-orientation and standardisation in favour of a focus on *process*. Each of us will work with the grain of our own developmental process. The practice and its transformative effects on us are their own reward, not merely a ticket to some other existence entirely.

Exactly what that reward might be depends on the level of our engagement. Many western meditators simply enjoy the peace, expansiveness and tranquillity of the practice. Others (insight meditators in particular) tend to be a little more ambitious and see meditation as a way of processing their lives, of maintaining a certain integrity, groundedness and sanity in the face of everyday difficulties, and not least during major transitions and 'life events'. Both of these approaches are skilful, in that they keep us coming back to the cushion and asserting a valuable priority in everyday life.

But we can aim higher still. We don't have to abandon terms like 'realisation' and 'awakening'; we just have to reframe them in terms of a process that can develop our individuality and human faculties – our humanity – to its highest pitch. We can become so much more than we already are, without becoming someone else.

In the previous chapter I introduced Richard Rorty's distinction between the paths of self-purification and self-enlargement. As he elaborates the latter, he paraphrases Freud as advocating 'becoming increasingly ironic, playful, free and inventive in our choice of self-descriptions'. We need to be more inventive in particular around the language we use to describe our practice and its effects. Rorty goes on:

> This has been an important factor in our ability to slough off the idea that we have a true self...It has helped us to think of moral reflection and sophistication as a matter of self-creation rather than self-knowledge. Freud made the paradigm of self-knowledge *the discovery of the fortuitous materials out of which we must construct ourselves rather than the discovery of the principles to which we must conform.* He thus made the desire for purification seem more self-deceptive, and the quest for self-enlargement more promising.[4]

In chapter 5, in Martin Hägglund's company, we found Marcel Proust and Karl Ove Knausgaard also deeply committed to 'the discovery of the fortuitous materials out of which we must construct ourselves' in order to 'own' their own lives.

In this context we'd do well to recall Martha Nussbaum's version of transcendence from chapter 1, a version that advocated deepening into the human condition rather than soaring away from it. We do that by nurturing 'a kind of precision of feeling and thought that a human being can cultivate.' We can thus realise 'a more compassionate, subtler, more responsive, more richly human world'.[5]

Perhaps *this* vision gives a more plausible and worthy account of 'realisation' than the conventional beyond-human one. We can realise the full potential of the human condition, rather than hankering for the exit.

To my mind, Nussbaum's words (quoted more fully in chapter 1) capture the highest aspiration we can bring to our dharma practice. She also nails the 'incoherence' in the conventional endgame model: it expresses 'the aspiration to leave behind altogether the constitutive conditions of our humanity [in favour of] a life that is really the life of another sort of being – as if it were a higher and better life for *us*'.

Realising and awakening as we practise

In the conventional models of dharma practice, 'realisation' and 'awakening' come in the final, crowning moment, which might be lifetimes away. In the approach to practice that I'm suggesting, by contrast, they're within reach the whole time. Realisation means 'realising cessation' (aka nirvana) – the third task (or third aspect of the fourfold task). In other words, it means *recognising* that we're temporarily entirely free of reactivity when this occurs (on retreat, say), and *experiencing* the expansiveness and peace it brings us. This is a reasonably common occurrence on retreats, and can greatly increase the efficacy of our practice. But we have to have our heads clear and our hearts open to know these moments for what they are.

Awakening can come just as readily if we set up the conditions for it. After all, it's a down-to-earth enough metaphor. Every day we experience the original phenomenon. We're asleep and oblivious, and then suddenly we're back in the world, with our bodily senses and brains on full alert. We can wake up to our amazing, scary, complex world, full of beauty and terror. It's available to us all the time, 24/7. But we usually don't see it because we're numb and jaded, our minds elsewhere. What if we really opened our senses to this world, gave it our all, as the Buddha suggests we do in the *Satipaṭṭhāna sutta*?

Stephen Batchelor couches his own answer to this question in terms of the *everyday sublime*.[6] Imagine seeing the stars (or the ocean or an orchid) for the very first time. This is what the Zen school call 'beginner's mind' – what bring freshness and vividness to our experience. And it moves us to the core. Here's Mary Oliver's pithy take on this possibility:

> Instructions for living a life:
> Pay attention.
> Be astonished.
> Tell about it.

Wondrous phenomena present themselves to us immediately and unproblematically every day; we just have to turn up for them in order to be transformed by them. Or as Dōgen Zenji put it: 'to be awakened is to be confirmed by the ten thousand things'.

Revamp: *writings on secular Buddhism*

Chapter 11

Forms of resistance to the inner life

I'm assuming that you the reader embrace the inner life. Otherwise this book would never have found its way into your hand. I imagine most of us would agree with Socrates in affirming the examined life as the only one worthy of a human being. What, after all, would an *un*examined life look like? Unfortunately we're surrounded by dispiriting examples of such lives in the public arena.

History and current mass media teem with the spectacular examples. The non-newsworthy ones follow a pattern: going through the day – or year, or decade, or lifetime – putting one foot after the other, doing what those all around as are doing; making habitual responses to the demands of the moment; choosing, acting, speaking (or shouting) without reflecting; avoiding ever asking where it's all headed; never evolving; never deepening or expanding; never tapping into a richer vein.

The Pali term conventionally translated as 'rebirth' actually means *repetitive existence.* Going round and round in circles. Or 'the wheel of life', as the Tibetans call it. And wheels going round and round a circuit make ruts. Now that really is something worth giving a swerve! Which is what the inner life – the search for meaning – is all about.

Meditation is just one way into the inner life. It can be entered in many other ways, too: walking in nature, listening to the sounds of nature or meaningful music, keeping a private journal, intimate correspondence or conversation with people close to us, spending time with (or producing) works of art, reading good literature, engaging in artistic expression ourselves, or even just living reflectively – including practising solitude.[7]

Perennial forms of resistance

The benefits of cultivating the inner life might make it sound like a no-brainer, but *resistance* to the inner life has been going on since time immemorial. Otherwise Socrates wouldn't have bothered pointing out the importance of the examined life. In Hannah Arendt's view (her Exhibit A being Adolf Eichmann), lack of reflection underpins what she calls 'the banality of evil'.

The Buddha dealt with resistance to the meditative process in one of his core teachings – already mentioned in chapter 9 under the rubric of the fourth focus of awareness – in the form of the five hindrances: craving for sense contact, aversion in all its manifestations, sloth and torpor, restlessness and anxiety, and shilly-shallying doubt.

Freud identified 'resistance' as the principal obstacle to the psychoanalytic process (yet another road into the inner life) as it manifested in free association. I'm pretty sure he was addressing the same problem that the Buddha did: the urge to skate along on the surface, no matter how thin the ice underfoot.

Early Protestant theologians even raised resistance to 'the inner probe' to the dignity of a virtue, and their legacy is alive and well today. If people looked inside and pondered their wretched chaotic lives, the theologians argued, they'd become terminally depressed, if not actually disobedient. To avoid that, the pious Christian should remain perpetually *busy*. God rewards busy people by making them rich – a sure-fire sign of His approval and blessing, went the argument. This was music to the ears of pioneering capitalists and their successors. So we find an archetypal busy capitalist, Henry Willcox, in EM Forster's 1910 novel, *Howard's End,* boasting: 'I am not a fellow who bothers about my own inside.'

We still live in cultures that affirm *busyness as a virtue in itself,* and those under its spell brusquely dismiss any form of reflection and contemplation. 'Don't ask a busy man like me to think about life, death, and the meaning of it all! Let alone sit around on a cushion doing nothing!' (The time-poverty of my fellow Sydneysiders is legendary.) All of us who meditate regularly have come up against this sort of attitude, and can find it difficult to justify ourselves in the face of it.

Another powerful form of resistance to the inner life is *distraction.* Consumerist culture – 'the greed and titillation society', as Donald Horne puts it – also self-evidently subverts the inner probe. In the case of the dharma at least, the inner probe depends on a degree of seclusion, distancing ourselves from jittery consumerism.

Before we go further into the problem of distraction as resistance to the inner life, we might pause to consider the superficial unattractiveness of the inner probe that fuels the resistance, given the human condition itself. Here's the great novelist Iris Murdoch's view of that condition, as summarised by the British philosopher and literary critic Galen Strawson:

> We are limited, imperfect, unfinished, and full of blankness and jumble. We [are] unable to domesticate the senseless rubble aspect of human life, the 'ultimately unintelligible mess'. We are divided creatures, distracted creatures, extended, layered, pulled apart, our minds are ragbags, as we struggle with fear and muddle (nothing is more evident in human life), with the invincible variety, the unmasterable contingency of the world, with moments of senseless horror and 'scarcely communicable frightfulness'...Egoistic anxiety veils the world. It sets up a haze of self-protective illusion.

The mind is 'besieged and crowded' by selfish dream life. It is hard to exaggerate our capacity for egoistic fabrication and 'rat-like fantasies'. We cannot see things as they are.[8]

Those old Protestant theologians had a point, then, didn't they? Choosing to spend time exploring this inner landscape demands a certain amount of self-confidence and intestinal fortitude. A meditative session isn't always a dance on roses. Fear and loathing of the inner world – of the mind itself – has become so intense that it has attracted a psychoanalytic term: *psychophobia.*[9]

Resistance in the digital age

Thanks to our sped-up lives and digital technologies, our distractedness has intensified further. In an essay in defence of an inner life under threat, Sebastian Smee writes: 'Today, being human means being distracted. It is our new default setting.'[10] And when we occupy that default setting, the inner life eludes us, making us different, drastically reduced selves.

To be clear: the new technologies haven't forced the recent change on us. The problem lies in how we deploy them and build them into our way of life – allowing them to become a bad master rather than a good servant. As a good servant they can help us achieve skilful purposes – witness the #MeToo movement, for instance.

But as a bad master, the new technologies accelerate our pre-existing resistance to looking inside and to acknowledging 'the whole catastrophe' that awaits us in there. It encourages our propensity to split off aspects of our inner worlds that we find painful; that don't fit some template or other, including our own self-preening delusions; or that we deem unfit for public consumption.

In the first instance, what we post on our social-media platforms masks our inner selves by creating what Smee calls a *performative self* – in many instances a performer desperate for approval and applause – not just in editing what is revealed or concealed about our reality, but doing so in the debased language that these platforms support. This is a language stripped of nuance, doubt and ambiguity; it consists largely of clichés, platitudes, stock phrases (often reduced to initials like OMG), emojis, and thumbs-up and thumbs-down signs. It's a language that lends itself to the abrupt, 'emphatic non-sequiturs' that typify social-medial utterances, such as Donald Trump's tweets.[11]

The tragedy is that over time we can gradually *become* these inarticulate caricatures of ourselves. They become naturalised. They become who we are to ourselves. Which is precisely what the owners of the platforms require. Those who use the social-media platforms constitute the platform-owners' *products* to be on-sold to advertisers. These products need to be reduced to the labellable and quantifiable units that can be factored into algorithms and targeted for micro-marketing.

We can link the art critic Sebastian Smee's alarm at what's happening to our inner lives to that sounded by the psychoanalyst Christopher Bollas.[12] He embeds his diagnosis of the inner life's current plight in a bold historical survey of successive, culturally induced 'frames of mind'.

In our digital age, he suggests, we arrive at 'transmissive selves' who melt themselves into various messaging circuits, and receive and retransmit so-called 'information', often intensively. There's no search for truth going on here, just the need to remain networked to virtual 'friends'. Which largely consists in sharing trivia and everyday logistics, and imposes conformity and the subliminal attitudes that underpin the process.[13]

Close friendships nourish our inner lives, yet we often allow our digitalia to disrupt them, too. Bollas illustrates this syndrome with a tragicomic scene in which he participated. Around eight friends meet for lunch at a café:

People arrived gradually in pairs and singles. Some did not greet us at first as they were deep into their phones, largely unaware of the actual world; others at the table were smiling softly into their groins, reading their text messages... The phones were enthusiastically passed around: photos of an event attended by some present were met with the usual exclamations – 'wow', 'cool'.

When we were all seated, and after the waiter had tried visiting the table three or four times, I came out of my psychic carapace and said: 'So, shall we order?' A glass of water was knocked over, bags dropped, alarmed heads popped up: I had verbally barged in on what in another era might have been a séance.[14]

People who are actually present are sidelined by those who are only virtually there. Becoming hyperconnected transmissive selves doesn't liberate us or add something to our lives – it *reduces* us, squanders our attention, and ties us to a standardised, hollowed-out way of being in the world. And of course, it militates against our delving into our inner lives.

The meditative life in the digital age

The Buddha thought it worthwhile to name the forms of resistance to the inner life that he encountered long before our complex societies and technologies arose. Maybe he was applying the strategy of keeping your friends close and your enemies even closer.

The rewards of pursuing a meditative life are invaluable, but we do need to be alert to cultural factors and new folkways that tend to obstruct our pursuit – as well as those on his original list. As many great meditation teachers have shown, the hindrances can be our teachers – they constrain us to look at negative aspects of the mind that we need to acknowledge and let go of. We can apply the same strategy to today's cultural obstacles, including those that deploy the blandishments of digital devices.

Chapter 12

Ask not whether it's true – ask rather whether it works

According to Friedrich Nietzsche, human actions, ideas and truth-claims merely express the individual or collective authors' needs and interests. Take an utterance like: 'There is one almighty god, and he has put me in charge of you; if you disobey my rules or disagree with what I tell you, he'll have you burn in hell forever.' The speaker is clearly defending or aspiring to his own dictatorial power.

Once upon a time in the west and the middle east, this sort of statement was common, and effective. Thanks partly to Nietzsche's influence, however, it doesn't work much any more in the west. We don't have to bother wondering if there really is an almighty god, whether s/he really did delegate authority to the power freak speaking to us, and whether there's a hell somewhere ready to receive the non-compliant. We can see that the power freak lacks the means to coerce us to get his or her way, and is just trying to con us instead.

The birth of the dharma followed the same logic of needs and interests. In the fifth century BCE, the agricultural revolution was in full swing on the Ganges plain, stimulating trade and urban life. Well-to-do townies like the young Gotama – and his first converts when he later began his teaching career as 'the Buddha' – lived high on the hog and enjoyed life choices (including intellectual inquiry) unknown to the vast majority still stuck in rural life. They expected that their advantages would keep them happy all the time, but instead they still experienced sickness, loss, ageing, death, and the other items on the Buddha's dukkha-list. Why was life so inherently disappointing and unsatisfactory, even now? They fretted over this fundamental existential issue.

Enter the new Buddha with his teaching of the middle way and the four great tasks in answer to their needs. He tackled the problem in a strictly pragmatic manner, without embellishing his teaching by embedding it in a cosmic narrative. In fact, he kept saying that the resort to cosmic questions and stories represented a significant obstacle to embracing the human condition in a meaningful way. As Nietzsche would do much later, he turned his back on all metaphysical speculation and truth-claims. Like Nietzsche, he really belongs among today's *post*-metaphysical thinkers, even though he's been dead for over 2400 years.

The Buddha concentrates on just how we can get *right inside* human experience. Both of them counselled against making up stories and theories about the human condition, trying to understand it 'objectively', as if we'd see it more clearly if we distanced ourselves from our predicament, and took what's called these days 'the view from nowhere' or 'the God's-eye view'.

If you watch television documentaries or visit airport bookshops, you'll have noticed that the view-from-nowhere brigade is still hard at work debating their opposing truth-claims. I touched on this problem in chapter 3. The view-from-nowhere reduces religions, spiritualities, philosophies and sciences down to their propositions – their truth-claims – and argues the toss over whose story is the 'right' one, that is, has the most defensible truth-claims. In doing so, they're missing the point: all these schools of thought are human artefacts designed to serve human needs and interests, just as the Buddha's discourses patently did. The real issues in the debate should be: whose and what needs and interests are being served, and how effectively? So let's follow the Buddha's advice and not get sidetracked into metaphysical claims and arguments.

Going by what we now know about the history and variety of religions and spiritualities – all those *social practices* – they've served a variety of practical purposes. These purposes include bolstering group cohesion; providing community-building moral codes and rituals; staging ceremonies for seasonal and personal transitions and life events; holding communal memory; and serving as a platform for aesthetic practices, a language for existential solace and reflection, and working hypotheses to satisfy humanity's relentless curiosity.

Religions are thus no different from other human innovations, like ploughs and buildings. Even religious ritual fits the mould. As Wittgenstein noted, humans are 'ceremonial animals', and this trait seems to constitute an evolutionary factor. Rituals help us to cohere in our communities.

The ability of religious social practices to serve their purposes does not depend on their myths being literally 'true', or even being believed. In the light of this usefulness, secularists might respect religion, even practise it in some sense, even though these days there are also non-religious ways of meeting these needs.

So what is Buddhist mindfulness-based meditation *for*, and what modus operandi does it propose to serve its purpose? Meditation keeps us focused on the fine grain of our experience, not least our *bodily* experience, and in this way leads us to 'fully know' and embrace what it means to be a vulnerable, mortal but aware being. What it means to be-in-the-world in this guise, in this way. To come to terms with our actual condition, instead of fleeing into fantasies of another set of preconditions than the ones we actually confront. That is, to ground ourselves in our real lives without 'craving'. This is the first of the Buddha's four great tasks.

We can find the modus operandi for meditation readily enough in the *Satipaṭṭhāna sutta*, among many other places in the Pali canon. Essentially it's about opening up the totality of our experience as it unfolds – in all its freshness and complexity – to awareness (*sati*); and over time coming to understand it (*sati-sampajāna*). It's *not* about being drilled to generate already-prefigured experiences while rejecting those that don't fit the template – which is the inherited agenda of formulaic meditation techniques.

Among other things, then, secular Buddhism aims to reinstate meditation to its earliest role as a major vehicle for tackling the four great tasks. To do so it promotes *non*-formulaic, non-technical insight meditation, in which one invites the senses and the mind to disclose their *entire* contents in all their layered complexity, so we come to see the whole picture, and gradually discern the patterns in our experience, in our individual way of being-in-the-world.[15] We need an approach to meditation appropriate to our actual way of life, not one appropriate to the way of life of institutionalised male renunciants.

To meditate effectively, all we need to put forward are our effort in following our immediate experience, and our honesty in acknowledging it. It makes no sense in this meditative environment to congratulate ourselves on being a 'good' meditator who can follow the instructions, or to despair and declare ourselves 'unable to meditate' because we don't experience what the textbooks prescribe. So many people quickly get a sense of lostness, inadequacy and failure when introduced to formulaic meditation that's touted as 'the one true way'.

The only real failure to note here is the failure to live like institutionalised celibates! And we're certainly not 'good meditators' by dint of often finding ourselves in blissful states, nor bad ones for sometimes seeing into the abyss when we're meditating. All lives contain tragic elements, and we have to receive them in our sits as we would any other experience.

We're all responsible for nurturing our own meditation practice, and the major issue we face is whether our approach is fit for purpose. The only true indications of meditative effectiveness are often subtle, off-the-cushion ones. Am I gradually strengthening positive qualities, such as friendliness (including to myself), empathy, generosity, clarity, self-reflectiveness, and equanimity? And am I seeing more clearly – and overcoming – my reactivity, immaturity and narcissism?

Conclusion

Already in the Buddha's own lifetime, some of his followers fetishised his teaching, his dharma, seeing it as a supreme value in itself, as the Holy Grail (we might say in our culture), instead of just as a means to an end. He tackled this problem in a teaching in which he compared the dharma to a raft that someone might throw together, out of any materials that just happened to be lying around, in order to get across a body of water. Having got safely to the other shore, what should the traveller do with the raft – leave it on the shore, or carry it overland on her/his head as something of great value? The ever-pragmatic Buddha strongly recommended leaving the raft on the shore.[16] It has already served its purpose, and that's its only value.

Stephen Batchelor suggests that secular Buddhists take this teaching to heart. We should throw together a raft out of what we have to hand in our own time and culture. The question then is not whether this is 'really Buddhism'; the only sensible question would be: does it float?[17]

Notes

1 Magid 2008; Siff 2010.

2 Anālayo 2003.

3 Rorty 2001: 154.

4 Rorty 2001: 155. My emphasis.

5 Nussbaum 1990; 379.

6 Batchelor 2015: ch. 9.

7 See Batchelor 2020

8 Quoted in Smee 2018: 37.

9 Bollas 2018: xiii.

10 Smee 2018: 55.

11 Smee 2018: 12.

12 Bollas 2018.

13 Bollas 2018: 43. He refers to the conformism of the transmissive self as 'normopathy' – being abnormally normal.

14 Bollas 2018: 48.

15 See in particular Siff 2010, and Magid 2008.

16 *Majjhima Nikāya*, 22.

17 Batchelor 2017: 106–7.

Part IV
Practising with others

Introduction to Part IV

Throughout this book I've adopted Stephen Batchelor's view that the dharma is a task-based ethical path inspired by a commitment to care for others as well as oneself. Ethics primarily concerns how we relate to others. In the first instance, the others in question are those closest to us, starting with our parents, children, siblings and close friends. They are the major contributors to our inner lives, too. As dharma practitioners we meditate and discuss essential issues in each other's company, hence other members of our practice community – our sangha – occupy an important place in our inner lives and our ethical development. The following chapter explores the history of this third 'refuge' (after the ideal of awakening and the dharma itself) at the centre of the dharmic tradition.

But any ethical system worthy of the name must encompass how we relate to others further afield, be they friends, relatives, neighbours, workmates, acquaintances or outright strangers. In the dharma all beings are interconnected, such that our care must include and go beyond our own species to encompass all of sentient life. In Part V we'll look at how care in its most expansive application ramifies into our civic lives.

The second chapter in the present section, however, will look at how we should care for an in-between group: strangers who are nevertheless close to us, not least strangers facing existential threats and thus in dire need. Today political upheavals and climate change are generating huge refugee waves which many stable, affluent countries are doing their best to repel with considerable violence. In this area an ethic of care is severely challenged.

Chapter 13

Sangha – the western dharma practitioner's dilemma

When modern westerners get a whiff of the life-changing value in dharma practice and decide to investigate it, they're likely to come up against traditional Asian cultures, beliefs and practices that are at first beguilingly fresh and exotic, but over time come to feel quite alien to them. This hurdle might tempt them to fall back on today's ascendant culture in the west that we looked at in the context of Charles Taylor's work reviewed in chapter 1: that of individualistic authenticity. They may have read about the principle of *sangha* (spiritual community) as being very important – one of the three central values or 'refuges' of Buddhism, in fact – but maybe decide it's surplus to requirements in the modern world.

After all, they may think, I have access to a plethora of how-to-meditate books and podcasts, and I can even download a meditation app. I can meditate by myself in my own bedroom, where I can also jump online and read or listen to any number of dharma talks. I can listen to dharma podcasts anywhere and any time, even while driving to work. If I want to talk to others about it, I can join an online chat room.

Okay, I understand that in other times and places people needed their sanghas because they had nowhere else to sit in peace and had no other access to the dharma. But it's not like that any more. Besides, I'm a busy person and can't afford to be tied down to a fixed weekly commitment (unless it's for something really important like football training). And finally, frankly, I'm simply not a joiner. Sorry. Two refuges are enough for me.

The weakness in this reasoning starts with seeing sangha as a mere resource rather than a process of being-with-others (in Heidegger's phrase) that is an essential ingredient of our humanity from day one. The feminist historian Barbara Taylor puts her finger on it:

> We become who we are through relationships. This 'I' is born at the interface of self and other, the helpless and help-giver, infant and parent. As babies we learn about ourselves via the minds of those around us; inchoate sensations take on shape and meaning through the responses of others. Selfhood surfaces on a tide of recognition: this is who you are/this is who I am. We human beings are dependent creatures who discover ourselves in communication with others, spoken and unspoken, conscious and unconscious. Without such communication the individual remains undiscovered, lost in a limbo of unintelligible being.[1]

So lack of community hollows out our inner life – confines us precisely to 'a limbo of unintelligible being'. Taylor introduces her bold statement with this one from her famous friend and sometime co-author, Adam Phillips: 'There is nothing...that can solve the problem that other people actually exist, and we are utterly dependent on them as actually existing, separate other people... [E]verything else follows from this.'[2]

Digital surrogates offering mediated communication simply don't cut the mustard here. In contrast *unmediated* face-to-face communication with others who are actually present is a rich, subtle and complex business. Meaning is communicated by words, yes, but also by gestures (including touch, perhaps), body language, tone of voice, facial expression, shifting direction of the gaze, intonation, hesitations, and so on. No wonder we find 'talking' among the activities of the body commended by the Buddha in his discourse on the focuses of awareness. There's a lot going on right there!

As against that, *mediated* communication (with the partial exception of audio-visual conversations) with virtual others is stunted, single-channel communication. The neuroscientist Susan Greenfield warns that we actually inhibit the development of our very brains if we habitually communicate with virtual others online instead of meeting up face-to-face.[3] Our brains need the complex challenge of unmediated interaction with others in order to develop physiologically.

So let's say we get past our two-refuges-only delusion, summon up our courage, and go looking for a sangha to join. Maybe we're looking for something traditional at first. Depending on which door we enter, we're likely to come up against at least two cultures starkly different from our own: elements of classical Indian culture preserved in most conventional forms of Buddhism, and the national culture of the Asian tradition we've lobbed in on.

We're likely to find that our new friends self-evidently believe not only in rebirth as a central tenet, and that everything that happens to them is caused by their past actions, but also configure their dharma practice around these ideas. We might find ourselves expected to bow or even prostrate before certain individuals, to treat authority figures with devotion, and to receive their utterances and directions uncritically.

If we stay with a conventional Asian-fusion dharma group, then we're likely to find ourselves split between two worlds – one that relies on all sorts of metaphysical and even magical assumptions and enacts hierarchical relationships including along gendered lines on the one hand; and on the other, our original milieu which upholds quite other cosmological and existential assumptions, and normalises egalitarian principles for how people should associate with each other.

It's not a question of one of these worlds being superior to the other. As I've heard Stephen Batchelor point out, the classical Indian worldview had a lot going for it. It situated human life within a breath-taking vision of a cosmos just as sublime as the one the English physicist Brian Cox unfurls in his marvellous TV documentaries. It instilled a sense of our actions today having effects in the future. With that, it also fostered a sense of humility, connectedness and responsibility, and set its face against egoism, greed and hatred. These ethical takeaways have never been more relevant than they are right now.

But today's natural science (evolutionary biology, Big Bang cosmology, neuroscience, genetics, big history etc.) and secular ethical thought do the same job.[4] When Charles Darwin was finishing his epochal book, *On the origin of species*, he was aware of the tension between his relatively banal theory and the magical narrative in the book of Genesis. So he ended his account of evolution by natural selection, with this comment:

> There is grandeur in this view of life, with its several powers, having been originally breathed into a few forms or into one; and that, whilst this planet has gone cycling on according to the fixed law of gravity, from so simple a beginning endless forms most beautiful and most wonderful have been, and are being, evolved.

The real question for us as practitioners is: which cosmology and reality-construct is most likely to 'land' in our own hearts and minds. The vast majority of people remain embedded in the cultures and beliefs in which they came of age. In these cultures and beliefs we are like fish in water – viable and effective in our native environments.

As against that, how many western converts can really make rebirth and insertion in a hierarchical lineage their very own without incoherence – as opposed to just paying them lip service?

The secular way out of the dilemma

A central argument of secular Buddhism is that we don't have to somehow vacate our own cultural foundations to practise the dharma. And we don't have to vacate the dharmic tradition to remain embedded in western culture. The Buddha himself lived and taught in a time and place in which classical Indian religious culture was not yet established, and his central teachings in no way relied on it. Major elements of that religious culture were simply added to his legacy after his death.

With the aid of modern disciplines we can now plausibly retrieve the Buddha's own legacy from the intertwining add-ons. We can do that without violence to it, and re-express it in modern secular terms. In this way we discover strong resonances between the early teachings on the one hand, and modern sensibilities (including pragmatism, scepticism and irony) on the other.

Gotama's teachings take us to the heart of our present-day ethical and existential issues, but they do so free of metaphysical presuppositions and beliefs. We can accept the invitation to his 'come-and-see' (*ehipassiko*) dharma while remaining supported by the culture we already live and breathe. His teachings can find a home here, and make of it a culture of awakening that flourishes in the secular age in which we live.

Inclusive egalitarian sanghas

All expressions of the dharma insist on the importance of practice in community. Meditation itself is a communal practice, current commercial adaptations notwithstanding. Meditation depends on our remaining in touch with each other: communicating with, caring for, and inspiring each other. Sangha (spiritual community) is the third of the three Buddhist refuges for this reason.

The term 'community' refers to a *process* of interaction and bonding between people, not to a mere sum of the members of a group. A shared purpose provides the focus for the interaction and bonding in question. The community's shared ethic drives it, and clarifies and supports the main ethical principles that its individual members each seek to cultivate and realise in their own lives. It would be odd if it were otherwise – we humans are herd animals, after all.

When we think about just how we should associate with each other in our sanghas, we find one of the most remarkable convergences of all between the Buddha's way of doing things, and the promptings of our own culture now.

His known world – the Ganges basin – consisted of two monarchies and five smaller oligarchical republics. The word 'sangha' originally referred to the governing council of a small republic. As far as we know, the members of these early sanghas met as equals and thrashed out issues in a freewheeling way.

The Buddha's father chaired one of these sanghas, and the Buddha seems to have admired the way they worked. So he in turn invited his followers into spiritual communities which took over the 'sangha' title and way of associating. As we've seen earlier, the form of sangha he recommended was inclusive – consisting of male and female converts, both mendicants and adherents. They were free and self-governing, not subject to hierarchical authority. They operated in a world in which spiritual discourse was free and diverse to the point of fractiousness.

This practice of communal life bears little relation to the way conventional Buddhist sanghas have operated over many centuries now, preserving as they do the monastic/lay dichotomy, hierarchy, and male privilege. But it does accord with everyday western assumptions about how to organise any voluntary association dedicated to virtually any human pursuit, from basketball and stamp-collecting to insight meditation. When functioning well, these voluntary associations exemplify that key area in western life – civil society. I will return to its significance in chapter 16.

Whether a sangha thrives or not is the responsibility of each of its members. It doesn't belong to a service industry and we're not mere customers: having decided to participate in it, we can't just grump about the quality of its 'services' to us and walk away. Each of us must own – and seek to identify and overcome – our sangha's shortfalls. They're not someone else's responsibility.

There's one final, important requirement: our sangha must have humour pumping through its veins. As we delve into our inner lives, we'll find plenty to laugh about. And remember to look for the 'aha!' moment each time you do have a laugh. It could be a vital awakening moment!

Revamp: *writings on secular Buddhism*

Chapter 14

Dharmic existentialist ethics in a time of pandemic

Today we find ourselves – like many generations before us, going back to the middle ages – in the grip of a deadly epidemic. Ours is called Covid-19; the earlier ones were called the Black Death, the Plague, the Spanish flu, Ebola, cholera epidemics, and so on. Some creative writers have used these occasions to plunge into their deeper human meaning; here I'm thinking particularly of Albert Camus's *The plague* (1947) and Gabriel García Márquez's *Love in a time of cholera* (1985).

The first of these novels comes out of the existentialist school of western philosophy which many see as cognate with the dharma. In his novel, Camus delves into what it means to live and work with others in the face of a mortal peril which puts everyone's life at imminent risk. Unwittingly he chose to write most of the novel in an actual community in which life was at imminent risk from another threat altogether. This circumstance intensifies the themes he raises. His novel thus bristles with dharmic resonances that I want to explore with you.

Camus, still well-known today for his contribution to existentialism, was a Frenchman born in 1913. By the time Nazi Germany conquered and occupied much of France in 1940 he was an established writer, and he planned *The plague*[5] as an allegory of the German occupation of his country.

The story he tells is set in Oran – a modern, commercial and uncharming city on the Algerian coast. Life here is extraordinarily banal, until rats in growing numbers start staggering out onto the streets and landings, and haemorrhaging and dying at the feet of the indignant citizens. Not long after that, a number of the citizens start dying horribly of a strange disease.

The novel's protagonist, a plain man called Bernard Rieux, is one of the city's doctors. He quickly drops to the almost unthinkable conclusion that this modern city is beset by a medieval calamity, the Black Death. The city fathers and several other doctors at first take umbrage at this suggestion. But the epidemic gathers speed, and the national authorities isolate the city to stop the plague spreading to other areas. No-one is allowed in or out, and for several months the citizens of Oran are locked in with the plague, which picks them off randomly and in ever larger numbers.

Rieux and his closest associates are ordinary, private individuals who make no pretence to heroism or public-spiritedness, and have a tendency to get lost in their own personal tribulations. But they are also realists; they react with irritation at the widespread denial and trivialisation going on among other doctors and officials. The logic of the truth they're bearing witness to gradually draws them into the dangerous work of fighting the plague.

This is a story within a wider story. Camus suffered from tuberculosis. Some way into writing the novel he's forced to leave Paris for a place with cleaner, drier air in which to continue writing. He moves to a quiet, poor, rural town of around 5000 souls on the French Massif Central, one called Le Chambon; he arrives there with no inkling of the drama that's unfolding in that town. But it's a drama acutely relevant to the themes of *The plague*, one that has left a clear impression in Camus's text. And the novel in turn has become a key source for those who've come much later to try to figure out what happened in Le Chambon.[6]

Le Chambon, authenticity and ethics

As the German occupiers in France and their Vichy collaborators rounded up Jews to send them to the death camps in Poland, some Jewish fugitives happened to turn up unannounced in Le Chambon seeking sanctuary. The locals – overwhelmingly Huguenots, devout Protestants – took them in, though it constituted a capital offence. As more Jewish fugitives arrived, the same thing happened. Jewish underground organisations noticed this pattern and began to send more and more of their desperate charges to Le Chambon. In time, the 5000 Chambonnais took in an equal number of Jewish fugitives in this way. No-one was turned away; everyone was saved.

In comparative terms, the Chambonnais approach to rescue on this scale was – to say the least of it – idiosyncratic. They had no weapons or organisation and very few resources of any kind. Church services were the only meetings they ever attended. Each family took its own initiatives, and seemed to believe not only that what it was doing was the decent Christian thing to do, but that any normal human being would do likewise under the circumstances. None made the slightest claim to heroism.

The Chambonnais were not to know that they'd now joined the tiny moral elite of just 0.01 percent of German-occupied Europe's inhabitants who undertook rescue work during the Holocaust. The vast majority of Europeans looked on as the Jews were slaughtered, refusing to believe it was happening, or refusing to believe that it mattered. This vast majority – including hundreds of millions of the Chambonnais' fellow Christians – had no respect for the truth.

Perhaps the most important characteristic of the Chambonnais was precisely their respect for truth – a characteristic that cultivating the dharmic eightfold path demands of us all. They readily acknowledged what was happening to the Jews, and they knew what the German occupiers and the Vichy authorities were like. So they rescued Jews openly, while flagrantly voicing their detestation of the German and Vichy authorities. They practised open, in-your-face spiritual resistance.

The Chambonnais knew what they knew, and they knew what they had to do about it. Their full acknowledgement of the truth made them stiff-necked and fearless; they had no reverse gear. In this way they stared down opponents with vastly greater firepower and no scruples about using it, but also no experience of dealing with people remotely like the Chambonnais.

Camus saw this drama unfolding, and we find strong echoes of it in his text. Right at the beginning of the epidemic Dr Rieux, has to contend with those who – just like bystanders to the Holocaust – refuse in the name of caution and prudence to acknowledge what is happening and pronounce its true name, because that would make heavy demands on the city authorities and disrupt the life of its citizens.

A certain Dr Richard fits into this category, and accuses Rieux of describing 'the syndrome' so as to make it look like the plague. To which Rieux tartly replies that he hasn't described a syndrome – he's described what he's seen (p. 40). And it didn't matter what you called it, if the authorities didn't take drastic measures, half the town would die. To quote the novel:

> But there always comes a time in history when the person who dares to say that two and two make four is punished by death...And the question is not what reward or punishment awaits the demonstration; it is knowing whether or not two and two do make four. For those of the townspeople who risked their lives, they had to decide whether or not they were in a state of plague and whether or not they should try to overcome it (pp. 101–2).

Decency, suffering and evil

As Rieux and his friends undertake their exhausting and dangerous work, they occasionally squeeze in a little downtime in which
to reflect on what they think they're doing. Here, too, the convergences with dharma practice are striking.

At a stage when one of Rieux's acquaintances, the journalist
Rambert, is still holding back and refusing to 'play at heroes', Rieux
replies to this objection:

> 'I have to tell you this: this whole thing is not about heroism.
> It's about decency. It may seem a ridiculous idea, but the
> only way to fight the plague is with decency.'
>   'What is decency?' Rambert asked, suddenly serious.
>   'In general, I can't say [Rieux tells him], but in my case
> I know that it consists in doing my job' (p. 125).

Like a good dharma practitioner, Rieux here refuses to talk in gen-
eralities. But it's clear from the thrust of the book that decency is an
effect of honesty – of acknowledging what is true and then acting
on it with whatever resources one can personally muster. Just as
the Chambonnais did.

Rieux and his friends exemplify the main original contribution that phenomenology and existentialism have made to our
ethical understanding, the concept of *authenticity*. It comes down to
the full acknowledgement of one's real situation; in contrast to bad
faith, in which one denies one's actual situation and the choices and
demands for action within it. Authenticity – being real in one's dharma practice – is an essential aspect of cultivating the eightfold path.

Naturally, the novel has quite a bit to say about our old
friend *dukkha* (anguish, suffering). Not just the physical agonies
of the dying, but the fear, grief and isolation that become the towns-
people's daily experience.

During the long struggle against the plague, a close friendship gradually develops between Rieux and one Jean Tarrou, a recent blow-in and something of a social misfit. Rieux is the type who 'keeps his own counsel', and it takes a long time before he opens up to Tarrou. When he does, he confesses that he only became a doctor 'because I needed to, because it was a career like any other, one of those that young people consider for themselves' (p. 98).

But as he practised medicine, Rieux has never been able to reconcile himself with death. 'Since the order of the world is governed by death,' he tells his friend and fellow atheist Tarrou, 'perhaps it is better for God that we should not believe in Him and struggle with all our strength against death, without raising our eyes to Heaven and to His silence.' And he intends to go on struggling against death, even though this struggle condemns him to 'an endless defeat'.

Thematically, the plague has now broadened its scope from being a metaphor for the German occupation, to being a metaphor for death, and ultimately of evil as such. That which denies and insults humanity. The struggle against death and evil – both embodied in the figure of Mara in the early dharma – will never be crowned by final victory, but it gives an individual's life dignity and meaning.

This wisdom impresses Tarrou. 'Who taught you all that, doctor?' he asks. Rieux's reply is instantaneous, and dharmically significant: 'Suffering' (p. 99).

Still later, Tarrou has his own confession to make to Rieux about his relationship with death as evil in pure form. His father was a public prosecutor. He was a good, affectionate father and Tarrou grew up very close to him. But one day when Tarrou is old enough, his father suggests he sit in on one of his trials to see if he's drawn to follow in his footsteps.

The young Tarrou watches the poor wretch in the dock

with growing sympathy, knowing his father is working to have him executed. When his father wins the case and the defendant is duly sent to the guillotine, Tarrou turns quite viscerally against his father, and against all the social institutions that create death. In Tarrou's words, which come very close to any dharma practitioner's self-instruction:

> 'All I know is that one must do one's best not to be a plague victim and this is the only thing that can give us hope of peace or, failing that, a good death...
>
> 'I have decided to reject everything that, directly and indirectly, makes people die or justifies others in making them die.
>
> 'That is why this epidemic has taught me nothing except that it must be fought at your side. I have absolute knowledge of this...that everyone has it inside himself, this plague, because no-one in the world, no one, is immune... What is natural is the microbe. The rest – health, integrity, purity if you like – are an effect of will and a will that must never relax. The decent person, the one who doesn't infect anybody, is the person who concentrates most...
>
> 'All I say is that on this earth there are pestilences and there are victims – and as far as possible one must refuse to be on the side of the pestilence.' (pp. 194–95)

Eventually the plague retreats from Oran. Healthy rats reappear, and people stop dying. The citizens rejoice in the streets as the first trains from the outside world arrive at the station, and the city opens its gates. But Rieux, nursing his own private bereavement, is not impressed. The novel ends thus:

> Rieux recalled that this joy was always under threat. He

knew that this happy crowd was unaware of something that one can read in books, which is that the plague bacillus never dies or vanishes entirely, that it can remain dormant for years in furniture and clothing, that it waits patiently in bedrooms, cellars, trunks, handkerchiefs and old papers, and that perhaps the day will come when, for the instruction or misfortune of humankind, the plague will rouse its rats and send them to die in some well-contented city (pp. 237–38).

To put the point about how evil endures – there is no final victory against it – and what this means for our practice, we can refer to the succinct terms of one of the four great bodhisattva vows:

Greed, hatred and ignorance rise endlessly; I vow to abandon them.

Notes

1   Taylor 2014: 203.
2   Phillips 2012: 73–4.
3   Greenfield 2008.
4   For instance Christian 2018.
5   Camus 2001.
6   Peter Grose (2014) provides a highly readable account of what did happen in Le Chambon.

Part V
Dharmic citizenship

Introduction to part V

The Buddhism we inherited from Asian sources already focused on individual redemption, something that made it welcome in the west as the latter's culture became ever more individualistic, not least after 'the psychological turn' in the postwar era. It appeared to be socially and politically neutral, even disengaged, particularly in its 'mindfulness' applications. They offered a balm for the troubled soul to anyone, including plutocrats, venture capitalists and similar speculators, arms dealers, and people engaged in other socially and politically dubious practices. Indeed, mindfulness promises enhanced efficiency in plying those occupations, as it does for any others. This social and political neutrality came with the ancestral Buddhist territory.

By and large, ancestral Buddhism – like other institutional religions – made a virtue of social conformity and political disengagement. It was the price its hierarchs paid for the continued protection and patronage they received from established socio-economic and political elites in the temporal sphere. These elites in turn relied on the political legitimation and mass subservience to their rule that the religious institutions delivered. (Until recent times, this symbiosis between institutional religions and temporal elites was also widespread in western countries, and still is in throwback polities such as Poland, Russia, and Latin American dictatorships.)

Yet, as we've seen in previous chapter, the dharma builds on a strong ethic of care. It resonates with the Christian 'golden rule' – treat others as you would have them treat you. It's also about acting generously, compassionately and fairly towards others, including strangers in need. It encourages solidarity with all beings, not just those of our own species, and concern for the conditions that allow them and us to thrive on our shared planet and in its biosphere.

In the light of the dharmic ethic of care, and the interconnected threats to the well-being of us all in today's world, social and political abstention is simply not available to the true dharma practitioner. If we care for all beings, starting with those closest to us, we can't turn our backs on the imperilled biosphere and those with whom we share it. Instead, we have to take on the active responsibilities of dharmic citizenship. This is especially so as we face today's two greatest (and linked) crises: the climate emergency, and the myriad social injustices that arise from spiralling inequalities.

These crises are intensifying suffering globally, and arise from organised human activity. We humans have even become a force that is changing our planet's physical evolution. For geologists and big historians it has entered into the geological epoch called the Anthropocene – the epoch of human agency.[1]

We must therefore shoulder the responsibility of overcoming these crises through our collective action. To shrug off this responsibility would be to admit to a grievous *lack* of care, and a failure to take responsibility for our own actions.

In 2019 the progressive (Catholic) Aquinas Academy in Sydney invited me to co-teach a course on Pope Francis's 2015 encyclical *Laudato Si': on care for our common home*. My co-teacher was the academy's director, Father Michael Whelan. As a dharma teacher, I found myself in the odd position of teaching Catholic doctrine to a class of socially active but religiously committed Catholics. To add to the incongruity, my day job as an academic had left me acutely aware of the main political lines that the Vatican has pursued over the last thousand years, and they've diverged markedly from my own inclinations. But I was also aware of the encyclical in question as a spiritual intervention into a now unavoidable political fray. It establishes a priceless precedent. So I jumped at the opportunity.

With this erudite and passionate document, Francis has made one of the most powerful interventions so far in the struggle against global warming. He has bridged the illusory gulf between the sacred and the profane to throw the weight of his moral authority behind the progressive side, while calling out the obfuscations and technological pseudo-solutions that leave the drivers of global warming unchallenged. In linking the climate emergency to the intensifying inequalities of the neoliberal global system, he is calling for radical change – to the consternation of conservative Catholics, among many others. As his subtitle insists, an ethic of care fuels his enterprise. In other words, he has published the sort of analysis and call to action that can inspire secular dharmic citizenship.

Hence the next chapter, based on my talks at the Aquinas Academy, consists in a dharmic response to the encyclical. The chapter that follows it takes the discussion of the need for radical change further. It asks: in order to enthrone care and responsibility in our societies, what sort of socio-economic and political changes are necessary and possible, and how do we envision the transition to a fairer and safer world?

Chapter 15

Defending our common home

For us humans, the next hundred years are really important...
Like it or not, we are now managing an entire biosphere, and we
can do it well or badly.
David Christian, *Origin story* (2018)

In traditional Buddhist spirit we can rejoice in the merits of all those dharma practitioners who mobilise in defence of our local and global environment – a defence that homes in more and more on a response to the climate emergency. We can also rejoice in the merits of dharma practitioners who join the struggle against local and global social injustice and human-rights abuses. Many of these practitioners would probably be surprised, though, to find the current Pope beside them at the barricades. He's an ally who unfurls another surprise by demonstrating that the two causes in question are in fact inseparable.

In 2015 Pope Francis issued his encyclical (letter) on climate change, *Laudato Si': on care for our common home.* The ethic of *care* announced in the subtitle informs the whole document and resonates deeply with the dharma.

This 'letter' – addressed to all people of good will, not just Roman Catholics – comes in at 183 forcefully written pages; it's a nice reminder of its author's previous career as a teacher of literature. Though it's doubtless the work of many hands, I suspect that

Francis himself held the pen as the manuscript took final form.

The encyclical draws on and skilfully integrates several bodies of thought and writing – the Catholic tradition, environmental and climate science, and modern secular philosophy. It represents erudition at its best. In terms of Martin Hägglund's distinction between religious and secular faith (see chapter 5), Francis joins the ranks of those with a self-evident religious faith but who harbour a strong commitment to what is at imminent risk in the world. So he exemplifies secular faith as well.

The literature on the global environmental crisis would already fill several libraries. Yet this encyclical stands out for three reasons. Firstly, the global moral authority of its author lends it wings. Secondly, it sharply criticises the many superficial and trivialising accounts of the crisis, and rejects outright the facile (usually technocratic) pseudo-solutions that distract us from the need for drastic change. Francis decries 'obstructionist attitudes' that 'can range from denial of the problem to indifference, nonchalant resignation or blind confidence in technical solutions' (paragraph 14).[2]

The third and most important reason this text stands out is its insistence on relating the environmental crisis to the great ethical failure of humanity today – its dire and intensifying social injustices and exclusions. The two crises link up and make up a dynamic unity, such that 'the human environment and the natural environment deteriorate together' (48). Here Francis's whole line of argument retrieves the central message of his lodestar, St Francis of Assisi: we must see care for the environment and the care for the poor as two sides of the same coin.

He thus makes common cause with other commentators who demand that we see the climate emergency in the context of other ills that have contributed to it and continue to exacerbate it. For instance, Naomi Klein points to the historic roots of the climate crisis, and of environmental destruction more generally, in systemic racism, colonial violence, and imperial rapacity towards the resources (not least the fossil-fuel deposits) of others – including indigenous others.[3] As she argues, the socioeconomic systems that originally produced these ills are still at work – a matter we'll return to at various points in this chapter.

Francis tells it as it is

The encyclical's first chapter deals with two general manifestations of humanity's abuse of the planetary environment: *pollution*, and *climate change*. Their impacts fall overwhelmingly on the poor. Let's review these two calamities in turn.

Pollution

This first calamity degrades local environments by littering our habitats with often toxic or radioactive waste, burying fertile, habitable land under mountains of waste, polluting our water, and destroying flora and fauna. Francis doesn't mince his words: 'The earth, our home, is beginning to look more and more like an immense pile of filth' (17).

Other writers have coined the phrase 'sacrifice zones' for areas destroyed through rapacious resource extraction – once-fertile areas that previously supported the communities, cultures and the ways of life of 'others' whom the plunderers shove aside and hold in contempt. Usually such sacrifice zones appeared in colonised lands, but the recent trend is towards despoiling metropolitan homelands to extract resources, not least fossil fuels, for instance the Alberta tar sands extraction in Canada, the widespread fracking in the English countryside and Oklahoma, and the huge new coal and gas projects in Queensland and New South Wales that Australian federal and state governments are encouraging and subsidising.[4]

Clean water is essential to life, Francis notes, so it's a basic human right. Polluted water causes epidemics of dysentery, typhus, ebola and other scourges, and it inflates the price of food. This pattern occurs typically in third-world countries where first-world companies plunder the natural resources of the poor, and extract them using toxic processes.

The same interests – deploying the alibi of 'modernising and developing backward regions' – displace established diverse agriculture and industry in order to produce single export crops. This violent process destroys the ability of local communities – not least indigenous ones – to support themselves and their ways of life. It often lays waste to the land and leads to the extinction of many species. Species that aren't mere 'resources' but have an intrinsic value to which commercial interests are blind.

In this way, Francis shows, the vested interests in question are 'making our earth less rich and beautiful, ever more limited and grey' (33, 34). For instance, by destroying diverse virgin forests to establish monocultures (39) such as palm-oil plantations. All in the name of 'wealth creation'!

Humanity's assault on the oceans involves both local and global damage. The local damage consists in pumping effluent and allowing artificial fertiliser run-offs into the water, and letting commercial fishing deplete fish stocks to the point of exhaustion and even species extinction. And we're warming the oceans, not just the atmosphere. 'Who turned the wonderworld of the seas into *underworld cemeteries* bereft of colour and life?' Francis quotes the Catholic bishops of the Philippines asking (41). As Australians watching the death agonies of the Great Barrier Reef, we're deeply implicated in this pattern.

Climate change
The second calamity – the climate emergency – *knows no national borders*. All of humanity shares the climate – it's our common good,

often referred to as 'the global commons'. When the atmosphere is assaulted, the damage strikes every corner of the earth, although (as we'll see) far from equally. As the ice caps and the glaciers melt, and the seas rise, untold millions face inundation of their homes and livelihoods, notably in third-world countries like Bangladesh and low-lying islands like Kiribati. A vast wave of climate refugees is already beginning to form.

Even in a rich land like Australia, we witness the rise in temperatures and the increasing frequency of bushfires, droughts and floods which, especially in less fortunate countries, is turning fertile land into desert. Forty-seven percent of humanity lives off the great rivers carrying melted snow and ice that rise in Tibet and the Himalayas to sustain the populations of China, and south and southeast Asia. Yet that vast frozen reservoir is rapidly diminishing, so putting us on notice of a yet vaster wave of climate refugees who can no longer live off those rivers.[5] Once again, it's the relatively poor who will bear the brunt of our carelessness.

The same is true of the much more violent weather 'events' – cyclones, typhoons and accompanying storm surges – that threaten third-world megacities built around river estuaries, such as Mumbai and Kolkatha. They occasionally strike their counterparts around first-world estuaries, too, such as New Orleans (Hurricane Katrina in 2005) and New York (Hurricane Sandy in 2012). In a third-world city straddling an estuary, untold thousands could drown in just one such weather event and the tidal surge it generates.

While climate change menaces us all, its current perils are by no means equally spread. As Naomi Klein comments:

> Although climate change will ultimately be an existential threat to all of humanity, in the short term we know that it does discriminate, hitting the poor first and worst, whether

they are abandoned on the rooftops of New Orleans during Hurricane Katrina or whether they are among the 36 million who according to the UN are facing hunger due to drought in Southern and East Africa (Klein 2016).

Decline in the quality of human life and the breakdown of society

In a vital move, Francis brings the themes announced by this heading into his account of the current environmental crisis. The destruction of our physical environment, including galloping unplanned urbanisation, goes hand in hand with a cultural and social breakdown largely fuelled by addiction to drugs and social media.

Younger generations in particular lose their sense of identity and mooring in functioning networks, starting with the family. These are symptoms of what Francis identifies as 'real social decline, and silent rupture of the bonds of integration and social cohesion' (46).

Nero fiddles while Rome burns

'Our common home is falling into serious disrepair,' Francis suggests in this initial survey of the crisis we're facing. 'We can see the signs that things are now reaching a breaking point, due to the rapid pace of change and degradation...[T]he present world system is certainly unsustainable from a number of points of view, *for we have stopped thinking about the goals of human activity*' (61).

Yet the global community's response to date has been markedly 'weak' in Francis's estimation. And this too is a cultural problem: 'we still lack the culture needed to confront this crisis,' he writes (53). Here his analysis converges with that of Amitav Ghosh in his influential book on global warming, *The great derangement*. If we don't develop a bracing culture in confident defence of our common home, Francis asserts, 'the new power structures based on the techno-economic paradigm may overwhelm not only our politics but also freedom and justice' (53).

It is time to look more closely at those structures and that paradigm.

The drivers of environmental destruction

Francis launches his analysis of the social and environmental ills that beset the world from an explicitly Christian ethical platform, which he calls 'the gospel of creation'. But it's one that dharma practitioners would have little argument with. 'The Bible has no place for a tyrannical anthropomorphism unconcerned for other creatures,' he writes (68). 'The Church must above all protect humankind from self-destruction' (79). 'The biblical accounts of creation invite us to see each human being as a subject who can never be reduced to the status of an object' (81). 'We should be particularly indignant at the enormous inequalities in our midst, whereby we continue to tolerate some considering themselves more worthy than others' (90).

Francis starts his third chapter, 'The human roots of the ecological crisis', by proposing that 'we focus on the dominant technocratic paradigm and the place of human beings and of human action in the world' (101). The technocratic paradigm thus becomes his central working concept in this crucial chapter, in which he nails the various destructive facets of the paradigm in question.

However – and without losing touch with his text – we might usefully unpack this paradigm as it manifests in our world today, and look in turn at the problems of technocracy, institutional biases, and market idolatry.

I have a backstory to tell about all this. Once upon a time in a land far, far away (Britain in the late nineteenth century) there worked a group of writers and political activists called 'the new liberals' – *absolutely not* to be confused with their polar opposites, the neoliberals who emerged a century later and to whom we must, alas, return.

The new liberals registered the astonishing rise in the productivity of human labour in the industrial revolution and posed the vital question – never posed before or since – 'What is industrialisation *for*?'[6] They answered their own question by suggesting that industrialisation was for raising all levels of society out of poverty and misery; meeting everyone's needs for decent housing, a sustaining environment, and health care for all; eliminating drudgery and bad working conditions; reducing working hours; and raising the cultural level of all social groups ('bringing up the rears' in their phrase). If they were alive today, they would undoubtedly add a stable climate to their list of desiderata for an industrialised world.

What's not to like? as one says these days. But clearly, in the light of the current crisis, the bearers of the technocratic paradigm have never liked the new liberals' message one bit. Let's see why.

Technocracy

Technocracy (a key term in Francis's working vocabulary) means rule by experts – both technical-scientific experts, and practitioners of disciplines that can underwrite power in given institutional settings, such as economists in key government departments and corporations. Francis draws our attention to the masters of certain key technologies in the world today: nuclear energy, information technologies, genetics, and others. These technocrats, he writes, now exercise 'an impressive dominance over the whole of humanity and the entire world. Never has humanity had such power over itself, yet nothing ensures that it will be used wisely, particularly when we consider how it is currently being used' (104).

Technocracy's self-congratulatory myth draws on the wider quasi-religious myth of 'Progress' which western modernity has always propagated. To put it mildly, Francis challenges this myth with some vigour throughout his encyclical (especially at 105).

Another story that technocrats tell themselves and other gullible folk is that their contributions are 'value-free' – they serve no other masters than Reason and Science. Thus their interventions and achievements self-evidently constitute Progress. Let's see if that computes.

Institutions and technocracy

Institutions are networks of power-wielding individuals united around a common purpose, which is to pursue a solution to a particular problem. Just how that problem is defined determines how the institution calculates – its 'forms of calculation' – and thus the impact it will seek to make in its field of operations. Today's policymakers focus single-mindedly on the problem of maximising national income, GDP, in broad accounting terms *without reference to* what constitutes it in the real world of goods and services, the damage done in its production, how it is distributed, and its relationship to actual human needs. As Robert Kennedy described this unidimensional measure of growth, 'it measures everything... except that which makes life worthwhile.'[7] It is touted as a measure of productive efficiency, but certainly doesn't begin to measure efficiency in enhancing human welfare.

Another word for these forms of institutional calculation – the one Francis uses – is 'paradigm'. As he argues, 'humanity has taken up technology and its development *according to an undifferentiated and one-dimensional paradigm*...[I]t is already a technique of possession, mastery and transformation' (106, his italics).

He goes on to point out that it represents what's usually called *instrumental rationality.* In other words, the decisionmaker is the subject, the decider, and other people and things are simply passive objects subject to exploitation, manipulation, exclusion or destruction, in the decider's interests.

For the rest of us who are impacted by the decisions in question, 'they create a framework which ends up conditioning lifestyles and shaping social possibilities along the lines dictated by certain powerful groups' (107). This is disguised power at its most opaque, least accountable, and self-interested worst. Experts become power-wielding technocrats when they operate in institutional settings and pursue the relevant common purposes in this way.[8] So they don't exercise their power arbitrarily, or according to their own personal ethics, but rather according to the forms of calculation embedded in the institutions they serve.

In fact, anyone working in an institution comes under pressure to *displace their own moral responsibility.* When we work in an institution, we attract praise, rewards and promotion according to how well we cooperate with others as a 'team player' to serve the goals of the institution, not according to our personal practical ethics. And the opinions of our workmates and bosses powerfully shape our own sense of self-worth. For instance, this displacement of moral responsibility was an outstanding feature of rank-and-file perpetrators of the Holocaust – men and women who were otherwise psychologically and morally quite normal.[9]

Today's crucial institutions and their technocratic mindsets

So what are the key institutions steering global development along its present catastrophic course, and what interests does their paradigm serve? Both emerged out of the neoliberal ideological wave that washed over the western world and beyond from the early 1980s. It initiated today's market idolatry and obsession with the growth of undifferentiated national income in complete disregard for social justice and environmental destruction.

I will have more to say about neoliberalism's provenance

and effects in the next chapter. But for now, here are its central nostrums – the elements of its paradigm – for 'progressive' national
economies and global economic institutions, as crystallised in 'the
Washington consensus':

- Market outcomes are sacrosanct and should not
  be subject to regulation or other 'distortions' (i.e.,
  mechanisms that redistribute wealth, income or life
  chances, or inhibit the exploitation of natural and human
  resources for private profit);
- National economies should be forced to open up to
  foreign trade and investment so that markets can
  perform their 'progressive' role;
- In the interests of private wealth accumulation, taxation
  and the responsibilities of government should be held
  to a bare minimum beyond national defence and the
  protection of private property;
- Since the way forward for all economies (supposedly)
  runs through participation in the global trade and
  financial system, there is no place for national
  development strategies based on democratically arrived-
  at social and environmental priorities.

This is a *hegemonic* paradigm: it promotes the narrow interests
of a tiny minority (approximately one percent of most western
societies), but it has been dinned into the public so effectively as
to appear as *common sense* and in everybody's interest.

Where would concern for our common planetary home fit
into this paradigm? The simple answer is *nowhere*. The paradigm
expresses 'an undifferentiated and one-dimensional paradigm' in
Francis's words quoted above – an expression of market fundamentalism that daily widens the gulf between rich and poor,[10] and

lays waste to the planet. Responsible economists have long since debunked the doctrine, but the dominant interests that it serves continue to uphold it as holy writ. It remains in their power to do so.[11]

The key enforcing institutions of the Washington consensus, all headquartered in that city, are the World Bank, the International Monetary Fund, the World Trade Organisation, and the US Treasury. Beholden to them are the major financial institutions (especially large banks) and stock exchanges of the world. They in turn impose a single criterion of success on corporations: maximal private profitability as reflected in the market value of their shares. The resident technocrats in this institutional pyramid are economists and financial experts – the ones who gave us the global financial crisis (GFC) of 2008, but who lost nothing in it and were never held to account for it. This neoliberal counter-revolution represents the triumph of financial capital over all other branches of capital, and all other social and human interests.

'Finance overwhelms the real economy,' the encyclical observes. 'The lessons of the global financial crisis have not been assimilated, and we are learning all too slowly the lessons of environmental deterioration' (109). In the same paragraph it goes on to debunk the usual neoliberal claims that market growth and technological progress will in and of themselves overcome both global poverty and environmental destruction.

It also points out the hypocrisy involved in doggedly sticking to 'certain economic theories which today scarcely anybody dares to defend' (109).

No wonder, then, that we find Francis asserting 'the urgent need for us to move forward in a bold cultural revolution' (114) to unseat today's dominant paradigm. He calls for the pursuit of 'another type of progress, one which is healthier, more human, more social, more integral' (112).

In the absence of Francis's cultural revolution we'll remain hostages of the Washington consensus. That fate will endorse the 1905 prophesy of the classical sociologist, Max Weber, who compared capitalist modernity to an 'iron cage' – an appropriate image for today's world in thrall to the dominant neoliberal paradigm:

> No one knows who will live in this cage in the future, or whether at the end of this tremendous development entirely new prophets will arise, or there will be a great rebirth of old ideas and ideals, or, if neither, mechanized petrification, embellished with a sort of convulsive self-importance. For of the last stage of this cultural development, it might well be truly said: 'Specialists without spirit, sensualists without heart; this nullity imagines that it has attained a level of civilization never before achieved.'[12]

'Entirely new prophets' are thin on the ground right now. But dharma practitioners are heirs to profound 'old ideas and ideals' that can be brought to bear on the present environmental emergency. It's our job to retrieve them and put them to work.

The ecology of daily life

The great majority of us make choices – about careers, job opportunities, what we buy, whom we bank with, and so on – as if we really were *homo economicus*, the self-seeking consumerist hero of conventional economic theory. But when a serious social researcher – not a market researcher – comes along, looks us in the eye, and asks us what we *really* find fulfilling in life, what's closest to our hearts, we list things like our intimate and family relationships, our close friendships, our work and workmates, our spiritual communities, volunteering with like-minded people, being touched by great art, safe living spaces, getting out into unspoiled nature as surfers, hikers, campers etc., and good physical and mental health. We can't buy any of these goods at the local supermarket. Homo economicus has gone up in smoke!

Francis sets out to exorcise the consumerist psychopathy that homo economicus personifies. Here he is at his most forceful. Because of our patterns of consumption 'we may well be leaving to coming generations debris, desolation and filth...We need to reflect on our accountability before those who will have to endure the dire consequences' (161). Well might we remember in this context the old truism that a society is a compact between the dead (who created what we enjoy today), the living, and the as-yet unborn.

Francis's 'bold cultural revolution' starts with that inner probe to bring our real-life priorities to the surface, to acknowledge them, and to act on them. Moulding a new common sense that actually computes with *and integrates* our common humanity, our spirituality, and our need to care for the environment that sustains us. This is at least part of the 'integral ecology' that Francis is calling for. It underpins his wider project of overcoming the overlapping crises of the environment on the one hand, and of social justice and inclusion on the other.

The encyclical lists many aspects of our current existence that call for drastic change as part of an integral ecology. It calls on us to create immediate living environments of calm and beauty, starting in our own homes, amid the noise, ugliness and brutality of modern urban life.

Many western cities (such as my own home city, Sydney) teem with examples of how urban pseudo-renewal and so-called development foster increasingly ugly cityscapes, ones overshadowed by the arrogantly soaring towers of finance houses and casinos. Back down at street level, urban decay breeds addiction, violence and criminality. New suburbs – tomorrow's slums – eat into rural land. They lack infrastructure and communal amenities like parks, sports grounds, meeting places, performance spaces, schools, libraries and public transport. People from diverse backgrounds move into these suburbs, but they lack venues and opportunities to meet and get to know each other, to integrate, and to foster a shared sense of local belonging enriched by their multiplicity. Accelerated individual consumerism offers no palliative for those deprived communities living in such soul-destroying places.

In third-world countries we can see the same forces of degradation at work, but the addition of poverty and extreme social injustice and exclusion intensifies the growth of criminal gangs, addiction and violence.

None of this is calculated to raise people's awareness of the wider environmental emergency, still less to encourage them to do their bit to ameliorate it.

Cultural ecology

Francis points out that the way most of us live now blinds us to natural processes such as the constraints of finite resources and the cycle of decay and regeneration. For starters, the majority of the world's human population now lives in cities. Accompanied by their parents, children can wander through the aisles of the local supermarket with no sense of where the milk, cereals, juices, seafood and meat come from – the farmers, the fishers, their toil and risks, the land, the floods and droughts, the seasons. Few of the supermarkets' offerings are 'in season' or 'out of season' any more; they remain much the same all year round, with no sense of scarcity. If oranges aren't in season here you can import them from the other side of the world. And so on.

What sort of culture are these children absorbing? Francis makes a telling point here:

> Culture is more than what we have inherited from the past, it is also, and above all, a living, dynamic and participatory

present reality, which cannot be excluded as we rethink the relationship between human beings and the environment (143).

He goes on to show how our consumerist, globalised way of life 'has a levelling effect on cultures, diminishing the immense variety which is the heritage of all humanity' (144).

Monocultures like palm-oil plantations destroy self-sustaining communities that once thrived on diverse agriculture and crafts. This process is especially egregious when it destroys indigenous communities, whose cultures exemplify how human beings can flourish in sustainable intimacy with the particular region they occupy, and the flora and fauna that they share it with. Neoliberal 'development' tramples indigenous peoples' rights to refuse resource-extraction projects – rights that the 2007 UN Declaration on the Rights of Indigenous People asserts.

We who call Australia home must take collective responsibility for one of the world's worst examples of attempted obliteration of an indigenous culture. It began with the slow-burn colonial genocide and dispossession, extended to child-stealing on a mass scale, and now finds expression in the government's graceless dismissal of the surviving indigenous people's poignant Uluru *Statement from the heart* from 2017. The 'rights' of mining companies and shareholders come before indigenous ones! We live on a fragile continent which our indigenous people have sustained and lived off for more than 60,000 years, and developed a culture to guide them in this custodianship. They want to tell us about it, but our rulers don't want to listen.

Here, I suggest, Francis is unearthing the underlying cultural dynamics that propel the destruction of the planet. He writes:

> Many intensive forms of environmental exploitation and
> degradation not only exhaust the resources which provide

local communities with their livelihood, but also undo social structures which, for a long time, shaped cultural identity and their sense of the meaning of life and community. The disappearance of a culture can be just as serious, or even more serious, than the disappearance of a species of plant or animal. The imposition of a dominant lifestyle linked to a single form of production can be just as harmful as the altering of ecosystems (145).

Embodiment and ethics

The phenomenologist, Maurice Merleau-Ponty (1908–61), criticised the mind-body split in western thought and insisted on the importance of the body in generating our mental life, most particularly our perceptions. In short, he insisted on the principle of *embodiment*. Like it or not, we're *embodied* beings.

Francis picks up this theme when he writes, 'our body itself establishes us in a direct relationship with the environment and with other living beings...Learning to accept our body, to care for it and respect its fullest meaning, is an essential element of any genuine human ecology.' As against that, 'thinking we enjoy absolute power over our bodies turns, often subtly, into thinking that we enjoy absolute power over creation' (155). By bringing us into a living relationship with our environment, our body also teaches us what he calls 'the moral law'.

This is familiar territory for dharma practitioners. In his very first teaching, the Buddha defined the first task of a spiritual practitioner as embracing and fully knowing the difficult aspects of human life, which (as we saw in chapter 1) he listed as birth, death, ageing, sickness, being separated from what we love, being thrown together with what we loathe, frustration, and our general psycho-physical fragility. Here are the great reality checks for our species served up by our very own bodies! It's where spiritual life

– the pursuit of meaning, starting with ethics – begins.

Among other things, our bodies teach us that we're interdependent, social creatures who wouldn't survive a day without the input of human and non-human others. So the moral law is about living responsibly on this earth, and about reciprocity – treating each other as of equal worth and equal vulnerability as ourselves. The golden rule of Christianity arises out of the conditions of our embodiment.

In a globalised world and its culture, this fundamental ethical teaching is easily lost. As we select a snappy t-shirt going for $10 at the local Kmart and take it to the cashier, do we pause to wonder what the cheap price is telling us about the working and living conditions of the person who sewed it in Dacca? We certainly should do so if we actually care for our fellow human beings. As we ponder the local K-mart's supply chain and our ethical responsibility for it, we might recall John Donne's words – one of the finest expressions of care in the English language:

> No man is an island entire of itself; every man
> is a piece of the continent, a part of the main;
> if a clod be washed away by the sea, Europe
> is the less, as well as if a promontory were, as
> well as any manner of thy friends or of thine
> own were; any man's death diminishes me,
> because I am involved in mankind.

What we can do now for our common home

To conclude this chapter I'll freely gloss chapter 5 of Francis's encyclical, 'Lines of approach and action'.

As noted, the encyclical affirms the obvious truth that our present lifestyle in rich countries would be simply unsustainable if it were replicated on a global scale (161). As poorer societies strive for our level and pattern of consumption, we humans will cook the planet even faster. But sloppy thinking about that truth can lead straight into deep pessimism. We can lose ourselves in such questions as 'How on earth do we persuade the less well-off to abandon their aspirations to live like us?' And: 'How do we persuade ourselves, given our living standards and habits, to give up some of our luxuries, conveniences and options?'

It would be easier, of course, if there were less inequality between and within societies. If the Joneses would only stop buying a new car every year and building extensions onto their home, we'd feel a lot less pressure to do likewise so as to keep up with them. That nasty little green hobgoblin of envy wouldn't come visiting so much, and we'd experience contentment more often.

While we're waiting for our governments to radically redistribute wealth, income and life chances more equitably and so bring our envy under control, there are more immediate things we can do. We can start to change the culture in myriad ways. For instance, we can minimise the use of plastic by not buying fresh food wrapped in it, and not emerging from supermarkets and department stores carrying our purchases in single-use plastic bags. We need to become the change we're trying to achieve in the wider world. Let's make most current uses of plastic socially unacceptable.

We could also stigmatise buying bigger-than-necessary cars, and driving when we could walk, cycle or catch the bus. We could make giving up car ownership altogether a praiseworthy act. In purely physical terms, changing our own habits and choices will do very little to ameliorate environmental damage. But when we contribute to *cultural* changes in the way whole populations live, our contribution can become much more significant.

Here's an example. In 2019 I spent two months in Sweden, home of Greta Thunberg, the teenage climate activist who

– among much else – criticised our profligate indulgence in air travel (a major contributor to global CO_2 emissions). The Swedish media were reporting a consequent drastic downturn in the sale of air tickets, cancellation of flights, and an astonishing rise in the sale of long-distance rail tickets. In response Greta herself coined two new Swedish words, *flygskam* (shame over flying) and *tågskryt* (bragging rights for taking the train). These words were finding their way into the English language before the Covid-19 pandemic put paid to long-distance air travel for the duration. A few years ago another useful Swedish word, *lagom* (just enough) entered our own language to good effect in much the same way.

More radically, each of us could stop thinking about our personal response to climate change in negative terms, 'what I must give up'. Maybe the biosphere is actually nudging us to *grow up* – to get a grip on our fundamental priorities as we found Martin Hägglund suggesting in chapter 5 – and thereby to exorcise our inner homo economicus, who is actually just an immature narcissist. S/he manifests all the character traits of narcissistic personality disorder: self-obsession, grandiosity, lack of empathy, rage (from 'the narcissistic wound'), and obliviousness to social norms and expectations. In Christian terms, the seven deadly sins[13] sum up the personality disorder in question. As any good clinician will tell us, these traits arise from a damaged or undeveloped sense of self, and condemn the narcissist to an emotionally impoverished existence.

So there are two more profound questions that come before the question, 'What must I give up?': What do I value above all? To what or whom do I owe my most fundamental loyalty? One way to get at the answers is to imagine what our priorities *as manifested in practice* will look like on our deathbed. I've participated in a course on death and dying in which one piece of weekly homework was to write our own obituaries, after our imagined death at any age we chose. What do we want to be remembered for? How would those closest to us recall our character and deeds?

Many of us might find that what really matters to us makes little or no contribution to our carbon footprint at all. In the process of this inquiry we might be turning ourselves around, to become deeper, more reflective and decent individuals.

Defending political culture and institutions

Francis keeps returning to the theme of threats to human cultures and institutions as part of the dual crisis he's analysing. He's not doing so in a vulgar conservative way of resisting change, but rather out of the sense that we become disoriented and easily slump into a dislocated and violent, selfish state of nature without our inherited cultures and institutions. We can't implement ecological policies without coherent and stable institutions. He writes:

> Here, continuity is essential, because policies related to climate change and environmental protection cannot be altered with every change of government...*A healthy politics* is sorely needed, capable of reforming and co-ordinating institutions, promoting best practices and overcoming undue pressure and bureaucratic inertia [181].

In 1964, Donald Horne dubbed Australia 'the lucky country', albeit in an ironic tone in a famous book with that title. One way in which those of us in this country are genuinely lucky consists in being the second oldest extant democracy in the world after Aotearoa New Zealand. We enjoy stable institutions of democratic governance. But to work well and nurture 'a healthy politics', institutional democracies need the support of a matching political culture – one consisting of robust electoral parties, practices and public discourse – that's also in good repair. Nowadays we're not at all lucky in that regard.

Over the last three decades our political culture has degenerated to the point where our democracy, like that of many comparable countries, is heading 'towards becoming something of an empty shell,' in Colin Crouch's words.[14] It barely functions beyond the rituals of general elections and tribalistic, ego-driven spats in federal and state parliaments.

Crouch explores this dispiriting development in his book, *Post-democracy.* In his account, three major elements have contributed to the degeneration of western democracy towards a post-democratic condition. The first element consists of a thick membrane – the political class – that has inserted itself between us and those who claim to represent us. It consists of the owners of the monopolised mass media; corporate leaders, publicists and 'influencers'; lobbyists and lobby groups (including ones posing as think-tanks); politicians' staffers, minders, spin doctors, perception managers and focus-group ringmasters; and most of the politicians themselves. With honourable exceptions, very few of these influential people have any interest in climate policy, and many actively oppose it as members of 'the Carbon Club', on behalf of the fossil-fuel industries.[15]

The politicians themselves are now increasingly drawn from the ranks of the staffers. And these days there's a thriving cash-for-access industry; if you want access to key politicians you have to pay for it by way of donations to his/her party's electoral coffers. The amount you donate governs the quality and quantity of access you get. Most substantial political decisions and deals are made behind closed doors either within the political class, or between its members and senior government functionaries. These secretive dealings between private interests and public authorities foster the corruption endemic to today's public life.

The second major element that degrades democracy is the corruption of public discourse and language, which has collapsed into slogans, managerial cant, boilerplate phrases, sound bites, bald-faced lies (in our 'post-truth' political space), and tweets.

The third element that has dragged us down to a post-democratic condition is the displacement of occasions for public political dialogue ('the democratic conversation' as it's sometimes called) in favour of 'media events' – events that are staged, scripted and choreographed to be televised, ones in which members of the public – if present at all – are simply voiceless extras in the movie. In Australia, media events typically consist of senior politicians visiting worksites wearing hardhats and protective eyewear, and uttering sound bites into the cameras and microphones. In the USA they often take the form of party conventions and rallies consisting mainly of hoop-la, caterwauling rock stars, and politicians braying emphatic non sequiturs Donald Trump-style to whip up their claqueurs.

Thus Francis's 'healthy politics' in which climate policy might gain leverage is conspicuous by its absence in many post-democratic polities. During the 2019 federal election campaign in Australia, for instance, polls showed a clear majority of voters understood the urgency of implementing an effective climate policy; and yet the election ended up returning a government with no climate policy and – in its patent subservience to fossil-fuel industries – has no intention of developing one.[16] This outcome exemplifies our post-democratic condition well enough.

The struggle for an effective climate policy to defend our common home is at the same time a struggle both to overcome social injustice and to restore real democracy in the interests of 'a healthy politics'. It's a struggle to sweep aside the membrane of the political class so as to make our elected representatives actually represent our interests. The struggle includes reasserting the authority of our civic institutions and the civil society with which we identify and in which we formulate and press for our ethical priorities in policy terms. I'll go further into what this remediation calls for in the next chapter.

We still have the vote, the right to assemble, and a fair degree of freedom of speech. So it's up to us. If we want to devise and insist on an effective environmental politics, we must at the same time restore real democracy in our several countries. We need to mobilise in large numbers in our civic institutions and movements, around well thought-out lines of implementable environmental policy. A dharma practice worthy of the name includes participation in this urgent effort, for the sake of all beings.

In the next chapter I will also return to Martin Hägglund's analysis to unearth the dynamic whereby the intertwined projects in aid of a healthy environment, social justice and the restoration of democracy might proceed.

Chapter 16

Transition

*Since anyone who criticises the entire systems of others has
a duty to replace them with an alternative of her/his own,
containing principles that provide a more felicitous support
for the totality of effects to be explained, we shall extend our
meditation further in order to fulfil this duty.*
Giambattista Vico, *La scienza nuova* (1725)

If we're to meet the challenges issued in the previous chapter,
so supplanting 'the dominant technocratic paradigm' that Pope
Francis calls out, we have to go deeper into the historical roots
and workings of that paradigm which I've already identified as
neoliberalism. As we do so, we'll notice that it functions on three
levels – as a quasi-religion, an ideology, and a utopian political
programme. I'll try to cut a long story short.

The story starts in 1776 with the publication of Adam
Smith's paean to market economics: *The wealth of nations*. A market works as an 'invisible hand' that miraculously aggregates and
transforms the actions of self-interested individuals into the op-
timal benefit of all, he argues. As he notes, humans have shown a
'propensity to truck, barter and trade' since time immemorial. It
was a handy way for human bands to swap what they had in abundance (particular foodstuffs, raw materials, artefacts) for what they
had too little of. They could do so more conveniently if they used

a medium of exchange, such as money. Nothing else needed to change for any human band (or whole society) that deployed this mechanism. Social structure, the inclusion of everyone in it, and the distribution of wealth and income that it mandated, could all remain undisturbed.

As a leading figure in the Scottish Enlightenment, Smith assumed that markets in goods and services would operate within and between societies in which 'moral sentiments', such as generosity and compassion, still reigned.

Fast forward to the first half of the nineteenth century and the industrial revolution in Britain, when influential political-economic thinkers proposed (and their powerful political friends violently enforced through state action) a whole new role for markets and money that displaced 'moral sentiments' entirely. Karl Polanyi tells this part of the story in his *The great transformation* from 1944. The thinkers in question proposed a utopia which upended the dominance of society over economy in all known human collectivities. Now the market economy was to mould society instead. To break down existing society and impose this utopia in its place, every productive element in society (land, labour, and even money itself) had to be reduced to private ownership in order to become a commodity, to find its price on the market, and sink or swim as best it could.

No more would anyone have a secure place – or even the means of bare subsistence – in this new *market society*, the utopia in question. All pre-existing forms of poor relief were abolished; the resulting social insecurity ensured a cheap, docile workforce, part of which was perennially unemployed in order to ensure 'market discipline' (that is, life-or-death competition between workers). The hordes of dispossessed rural workers streaming into the cities faced the stark choice between taking any factory job they were offered – under atrocious and dangerous working conditions – or see their families living on the street and starving. Greed and fear would propel economic behaviour, and crowd out moral sentiments. Such was (and remains) the essential political programme of economic liberalism, of which today's neoliberalism is merely the most recent iteration.

To the variable extent to which economic liberals have succeeded, their programme has spawned a dynamic that includes ever widening inequalities, endemic unemployment, and social exclusion. On the 'positive' side – and on the back of unimaginable human suffering at home and abroad – it has created the industries, technologies and excess that we in the rich countries witness today.

At the religious level, economic-liberal doctrine presented (and still presents) the market, with its omniscient and beneficent 'invisible hand', as an object of monotheistic faith and idolatry, instead of just a pragmatic mechanism for the exchange of goods and services as it was for Adam Smith. Everyone must submit to its will. At the ideological level, all the market's mechanisms and outcomes, and the alienation of society's productive resources into private hands, were held out as *natural*, and thereby non-negotiable. The market itself and private ownership of society's resources (so the myth goes) have existed since time immemorial, and to interfere with them would lead to political tyranny and economic misery – the wages of blasphemy. (Actual history tells a different story: markets and private property in social resources are historical aberrations – politically conceived institutions violently imposed, hardly eternal ones ordained by God or nature.)

As a political programme, economic liberalism thus sought to restrict the role of the state to acting as a 'nightwatchman', defending the realm from foreign threats, and buttressing private property rights at home. It thus opposed all but minimal taxes, and all attempts to restrain the exercise of private ownership rights in the pursuit of maximal private profits. All regulation of working conditions and the environmental impacts of commercial activity were (and remain) sacrilegious to the one true faith of economic liberalism. As were measures to redistribute income and provide social relief for the unemployed and indigent, all of which compromised market outcomes and private prerogatives.

Economic liberals have not always been successful in defending their pure model on these points, but they have by and large continued to impose a narrow conception of the state's responsibilities, *and thus a narrow ambit for democratic decision-making*. This has insulated the exercise of private ownership prerogatives in the economy from democratic deliberation and policy. We can identify the rise of the political class and its symbiosis with large corporations in the current neoliberal era (discussed in the previous chapter) as the insertion of yet another layer of insulation to shield the state from popular demands.

The economic-liberal utopia required a global reach. Beginning in the nineteenth century, western companies that had mechanised and grown large at home, thanks to governmental protection and favouritism in their infant years, could then plunder and privatise resources far afield, disrupt economic development in their colonised territories, and force their inhabitants to buy their goods. Thus another layer of enduring dispossession, misery and inequality was added to the one already imposed at home in the metropolitan countries, and an exciting new doctrinal product – free trade – could be exported on naval warships.

Free trade in practice facilitated the entry of the products of slave labour (from the USA and the Caribbean, for instance) into the supply chains of major industries at home, like British textile manufacturing. The dynamic of underdevelopment thus established remains on foot today in many third-world countries, as does slavery itself.[17]

Needless to say, such a destructive utopian programme, imposed by the state, met resistance from those who sought to protect society from it. The resistance included conservative push-back from churches[18] and other defenders of the older moral order. On the radical side, organised labour, democrats, socialists, the women's movement, collectivist or 'social' liberals (such as the 'new liberals' I referred to in the previous chapter) and other popular movements emerged to enter the lists in what Polanyi lumps together as 'the self-protection of society'. But unlike their economic-liberal opponents, the protectors of society have never united around one clear, simplistic programme.

In this way Polanyi identifies the enduring fundamental divide in western politics – that between economic liberalism in its various iterations on the one hand, and movements asserting social values, needs and interests on the other. In my view, it's important for dharma practitioners, who participate in movements to defend the biosphere or promote social justice, to orient themselves in this fundamental divide, so they know what they're up against and have to overcome.

The original economic-liberal blueprint assumed that representative government would provide the necessary political undergirding. Men of property (a small minority of the adult population) alone would exercise the vote and so constitute those to be represented. Hence the gradual spread of voting rights in many western countries became a complicating factor for economic liberals. They faced a huge problem: under democratic conditions, how do you stop the propertyless vast majority electing parties intent on moving against the assets and incomes of the tiny propertied minority? The parties of economic liberalism developed dark arts to head off this catastrophe, such as suppressing electoral participation (still a popular ruse among US Republicans), and actual or threatened capital strikes and flights to punish a recalcitrant electorate with mass unemployment.

But the most successful defence mechanism has been the ideological one. With the aid of conventional economic theory and fundamentalist Christian doctrine, and in spite of the evidence, the nostrums of economic liberalism have been rebadged as 'common sense'. In the same way that an alchemist turns base metal into gold, the special interests of the tiny rich minority become the interests of us all in a *hegemonic* ideology which finds general acceptance in this way. 'What is good for General Motors is good for the United States', as a later slogan had it. Taxation and regulation kill enterprise and retard growth; if people aren't forced to work by the threat of starvation, then they won't work at all. And so on.

The fortunes of each side of the great divide in western politics have waxed and waned to this day. Against fierce economic-liberal opposition, some progressive measures – such as minimal widows' and aged pensions – emerged before the second world war. But the war itself temporarily weakened economic-liberal parties, and for around thirty years they seemed to have suffered an enduring eclipse.

In western Europe and Australasia progressive governments representing the labour movement established welfare states that offered unemployment and disability benefits, old-age pensions, free education and health care. The process of intensifying inequality stalled. Some version of these boons even appeared in the USA. At the other end of the spectrum, in Scandinavia, welfare arrangements advanced to the point where thinkers began to speculate that a qualitative social change was underway to 'welfare capitalism', one based on the principle that every *citizen* enjoyed a right to a reasonable claim on the wealth and income that her or his society generated, such that s/he became a genuinely free, autonomous agent no longer coerced by the threat of starvation.

This is what true freedom came to *mean*: the individual's

ability to make life choices unconstrained by the ever-present threat of penury and social exclusion that inhere in economic-liberal arrangements, wherein only buyers and sellers exist – not citizens.

In his influential 1949 essay, 'Citizenship and social class', TH Marshall saw the citizenship principle spreading from the political sphere (where adults now had a right to cast a vote in elections) to the social sphere, where they had a right to *social security* – the unconditional right to participate in available social amenities regardless of class, gender, race and personal misfortune. Social security is an essential precondition for any individual's autonomy and freedom.

Scandinavian writers like Walter Korpi and Gøsta Esping-Andersen contemplated the myriad rights that working people had won (centrally-bargained equitable wage rates; job safety provisions; meaningful unemployment benefits; a say in job organisation) and saw them as 'de-commodifying' labour, in direct defiance of economic-liberal principles. Working people were now to be rights-bearing industrial and economic citizens, not just rightless hirelings. Governments armed with Keynesian demand-management tools committed themselves to maintaining full employment, something that bolstered the rights of labour, to the shrill denunciation of economic liberals.

But 'welfare capitalism' suffered from a fatal weakness: it was still capitalism. Production of most goods and services rested on private ownership and control of the means of production, and the 'welfare' component depended on the redistribution of wealth and income generated in an unchanged, privately controlled production system. In the stagflation of the 1970s the parties of labour wobbled in their loyalty to welfare capitalism, and then precipitately converted to a new iteration of economic liberalism – neoliberalism.

With astonishing speed, under the auspices of the conterminous administrations of Ronald Reagan and Margaret Thatcher in the 1980s, neoliberalism established itself as the (almost) undisputed basis of public-policy formation in the west. 'There is no alternative,' Thatcher announced in a famous self-fulfilling prophecy – one borrowed from Herbert Spencer, a leading nineteenth-century economic liberal. 'There's no such thing as society. There are individual men and women and there are families,' she also declared, putting paid to any appeals to social interests on her watch, and that of her ideological successors.

Since then neoliberals of the centre-left (such as Tony Blair and 'New Labour' in the UK) and the centre-right (former conservative parties) have set about dismantling welfare capitalism and reinstating the 'discipline' of social insecurity by using four main mechanisms: deregulation; defunding and privatisation of social services; and globalisation. Deregulation restores unfettered private-ownership prerogatives over society's productive resources. Social services were abolished or defunded to the extent it was politically possible. Social services that had become too popular to destroy outright in this way (such as Britain's National Health Service) were privatised piecemeal. Now a hospital bed or a room in an aged-care facility no longer served a social function, but became a privately owned asset to be managed as cheaply as possible and rented out for maximal profit.[19]

Globalisation – a political project that neoliberals, true to form, dress up as a natural phenomenon – allowed western manufacturing firms to dispense with higher-paid workforces at home so as to take full advantage of overseas low-cost labour in unregulated labour markets. It also forced third-world countries to comply with the rules of the Washington consensus (mentioned in the previous chapter). These rules blocked them from adopting national development strategies that met their domestic social aspirations, while forcing them to act as passive markets for western goods.[20]

Today economic liberalism has never come closer to re-alising its utopia of market society that it first announced nearly two centuries ago. As Pope Francis and thousands of other commentators have shown, the costs in terms of global environmental destruction and social injustice are on display in plain sight, and in spate. 'Climate change isn't just about things getting hotter and wetter,' Naomi Klein observes. 'Under our current economic and political model, it's about things getting meaner and uglier.'[21]

Such are the origins and effects of the neoliberal counter-revolution – Pope Francis's unidimensional 'technocratic paradigm' that is now despoiling the planet and threatening the very biosphere that sustains us. Many journalists and other writers have taken to referring to our current social system as 'neoliberal capitalism', as if it – like the 'welfare capitalism' that preceded it – represents a new kind of social system. Be that as it may, all social systems arise, endure for a while, and pass away – an observation that won't come as a surprise to dharma practitioners.

What can we do to make neoliberal capitalism pass away, and give way to something survivable and ethically sustainable (even inspiring), before it's too late? I'll return to that central question in a moment. In the meantime, we need to analyse neoliberal capitalism a little further to understand how a strategy for change might work.

What is to be transformed

In an important sequel to his *Post-democracy*, one called *The strange non-death of neoliberalism,* Colin Crouch (an emeritus professor of public management) contemplates how the doctrine in question survived the socioeconomic calamity it triggered in the global financial crisis (GFC) of 2008–9.[22] The major banks, whose mis-behaviour caused the collapse in the deregulated financial sector that they themselves had clamoured for, actually went on to turn their train wreck into a heist.

In the midst of the crisis, the banks told the governments in the USA and UK (neoliberalism's heartlands) that they were 'too big to fail'. They demanded financial handouts in eye-watering amounts from the public purse to stay afloat if even more mayhem were to be avoided. Once the governments had paid up, neoliberal pundits then demanded that the shocking new levels of public debt so incurred be paid for by renewed attacks on social expenditure on education, health, income support and social amenities. Such were the 'austerity' programmes visited upon the vast majority, not least in the UK, while the perpetrators entirely avoided being held to account, and went on to increase their self-awarded bonuses, as well as their political clout in deflecting calls for financial regulation intended to prevent similar collapses in the future.

On the previous occasion when economic-liberal governance caused a comparable international socio-economic calamity, in the Great Depression of the 1930s, it triggered diverse political knock-on effects in opposition to this orthodoxy. They included the rise of Keynesian thought and policymaking in the stable democracies, as well as re-energised fascist and communist movements in the more fragile polities. But apart from short-lived protests, such as the Occupy movement, neoliberalism emerged from its GFC still unchallenged as the basis of economic-policy formation in the west.

In analysing this strange outcome, Crouch comes up with valuable insights about western public life that can guide activists' approach to reform. He refutes the widespread perception – one shared by neoliberals and even many of their opponents – that the central conflict in public life is that between 'the market' and 'the state'. Neoliberal governance increasingly relies on entities of a third type – large corporations – which manipulate both markets and governments, just as the big banks did in the GFC and its aftermath. The state, the market and big corporations harmonise in a 'comfortable accommodation' to dominate society along amoral neoliberal lines, largely free of democratic inputs under the current post-democratic condition discussed in the previous chapter.

However, jointly and severally, these three entities are vulnerable to citizens' mobilisation that constitutes a fourth element in western public life – *civil society*. The ancient Greeks called this vital public realm the *polis,* wherein citizens came together to discuss and make decisions about public matters. What concerns the public should be transacted in public and by the public – such was its guiding principle.

Today civil society consists of a wide variety of self-mobilising citizens' organisations that articulate ethical values as well as special interests. It comprises religious and spiritual communities; unions; professional and other vocational groups; cooperatives; rank-and-file party branches; sporting bodies; and voluntary associations that combat racism and sexism, and defend the environment, refugees, the disabled, minorities, and the disadvantaged at home and abroad.

The state is vulnerable to these groups because they influence how people vote and can attract media attention when they organise demonstrations and publicise the transgressions of politicians and corporate elites. Corporations are vulnerable directly through the way civil society influences economic and political behaviour, and indirectly in forcing deviations from neoliberal orthodoxy. That public education, public health, public broadcasting and other social amenities have survived – however diminished – in most western countries through three decades of neoliberal attack is a tribute to citizens' mobilisation in civil society, 'the power of the powerless'.

Given the increasing salience of both large corporations and civil society in public life today, Crouch argues, the conflict between them is now the main event in western politics, not least in climate politics. The primary conflict is no longer that between states and markets, as neoliberal publicists would have us believe for demagogic purposes.

At base – and not surprisingly – today's neoliberal entities have inherited economic liberalism's original legitimacy problem; it's endemic in their antisocial rapacity and environmental destructiveness. Corporations have long tried to solve the problem by making a pretence to being something other than the single-minded profiteers and rent-seekers that their forms of calculation force them to be. In the 1930s 'the soulful corporation' was born, as large firms claimed to have outlived and outgrown their robber-baron founders, and supposedly high-minded, socially-conscious professional managers took over in a 'managerial revolution'. Today this PR effort has produced and routinised something called 'corporate social responsibility' (CSR) that highlights 'sustainable development', 'diversity', and other noble values, ones that firms unfurl on their websites and in their prospectuses. Though CSR remains essentially window dressing, it turns into a stick with which investigative elements of civil society can beat corporations when they violate their own CSR pieties.[23]

Crouch's advice to progressive activists is to stop concentrating solely on changing the direction of state policy – a still necessary albeit thankless task under post-democratic conditions – and to focus more on the leverage that civil society offers:

> There is no need for defeatism. Rarely before in human history has there been so little deference shown to authority, so much demand for openness, so many cause organizations, journalists and academics devoting themselves to criti-

cizing those who hold power and holding up their actions to scrutiny. New electronic forms of communication are enabling more and more causes to express themselves in highly public ways.[24]

Civically active dharma practitioners can take heart from this insight. At the same time, they need to see the limitation in the strategy behind it, which is one of mere alleviation. It assumes the continuation of neoliberal capitalism, and that the struggle will always limit itself to ameliorating the system's inbuilt destructive drives. This strategy leaves those very drives still in play. The earth and its creatures will never be safe while the institutions of the Washington consensus and Wall Street's and the City of London's kleptocrats continue to dictate the basic settings for economic activity – notwithstanding the temporary gains that activists in civil society achieve.

However, this public realm is the ground on which citizens mobilise spontaneously and in large numbers. It's also the answer to the conundrum that Machiavelli analysed over four centuries ago. Those who fight for political freedom must assemble a force capable of overcoming the reigning tyranny. But political freedom is only possible when power is dispersed.[25] So the means used to overthrow tyranny must also achieve a dispersal of power. Multifarious power bases – with newcomers constantly forming – already comprise civil society.

What if we in civil society were to pursue a higher goal – that of reversing the original abandonment of social resources to private ownership and self-interested forms of calculation under economic-liberal auspices, and instead aim to put society back in charge of deploying its own productive resources and redistributing the wealth they generate according to an ethic of care, generosity and fairness? Would not such a systemic change choke off the current destructive drives at source? And how would such a transition work?

From neoliberal capitalism to democratic socialism

Karl Marx posed the issue of transition – social-systemic change – particularly clearly. Throughout recorded history, he wrote, human collectivities have exhibited a number of identifiable *modes of production*, that is, core social relationships that govern the production and distribution of the material necessities of life. A mode of production is a pure model or 'ideal type'; any given society at any one time might combine various modes of production, though one will predominate. Over time, a predominant mode of production in dynamic societies will create the material conditions that necessitate and support its own replacement by a new one.

The main modes of production Marx discerned over recorded history are 'primitive communism' (hunter-gatherer communities), slavery, feudalism, and capitalism. The last three modes of production generated class societies, whose ultimately self-destructive dynamism subverted the relationship between the major classes involved, such as lords and serfs in feudal societies.

Writing during the industrial revolution, he celebrated capitalism's unleashing the hitherto unimaginable productivity of human labour in conjuring forth material goods through new ways to organise work and new technologies. But the system was in itself crisis-prone, and it produced not only material goods in abundance, but also its own 'gravediggers' – an ever greater proportion of the population that was ever more highly skilled, but held no productive property, had no say in its deployment, and survived on wages and salaries it had to wring out of the recalcitrant but shrinking minority of capital owners.

Through its productivity, instability and gross inequity, Marx suggested, the capitalist mode of production generates the preconditions for the transition to a successor mode of production – socialism – in which ownership and control of a society's productive resources would return to the members of that society, and classes would erode because they would no longer have any place in the new way in which the economy was organised.

Be it noted that Marx never at any stage suggested that the state should stand in for society in controlling the means of production. In fact, he strongly suggested the opposite – that the state would 'wither away' for want of a role in a society no longer riven by class conflict. In its place democratic precepts for human cooperation had to find a home in *all* institutions in which economic decisions are made and work is organised, otherwise society as such would once again be denied control over its own productive resources.

In his critique of capitalism, Marx made another fundamental point that should exercise spiritual practitioners today. Just as the capitalist mode of production requires the alienation of society's productive resources to a property-owning minority, so it demands that each employee alienate her time, creativity and energy during working hours to her employer.

Whether we're hunter-gatherers or geeks working for a tech company, we all have to work to earn our keep and stay alive. Most of the time we'd prefer that work to be in an occupation we've chosen ourselves, and to perform it under conditions we've helped to set up. It would be work we can express ourselves in, and identify with as a meaningful process with a satisfying outcome. In this way our working lives would express our secular faith and clinch our spiritual freedom, in Martin Hägglund's terms we reviewed in chapter 5.

But if we've sold our work-time – a major part of the overall time we'll ever have at our disposal – to a boss or large corporation, we lose all those features because our labour, too, has now been *alienated*. We've rented out our minds and bodies for the duration, and are no longer spiritually free in the sense explored in chapter 5. We neither control the process nor own the product. In fact, we're probably spending much of our working life creating economic value that goes straight into the boss's pocket, and engaging in processes that despoil the environment or otherwise affront our values.

So capitalism steals our one ultimately finite and irreplaceable resource, as Martin Hägglund explains it: our *time*. On that note, we can return to the second part of his book, *This life,* where he adopts Marx's theory of alienation, and follow the implications of capitalism in our spiritual lives. The temporal dimension encompasses our lives, and it also defines our possibilities. If we're to achieve spiritual freedom we have to set our own priorities in what we do with our time and energy, and participate in democratic processes which set our society's economic priorities and the forms in which they're to be pursued. Under capitalism, we're shut out of all of these processes, leaving us spiritually unfree and the biosphere in jeopardy.

Like TH Marshall before him, Hägglund pits the concept of citizenship against the capitalist order. Being a citizen is a practical identity to be sustained by all adults, so our working lives and the economic arrangements and developments that govern them are part and parcel of our spiritual lives.[26] We must 'own' all the questions raised by our work and its context, and democratic socialism would be the only mode of production that would allow us to deliberate on and decide these questions together with our fellow citizens. In this way it becomes 'a spiritual cause'.[27]

The word 'socialism' tends to frighten the horses, so a few points need clarification before we turn to how a socialist transition might work. Hägglund discards the notion of state socialism for obvious historical reasons, ones exemplified by oppressive Soviet-style societies in which an oligarchical *nomenklatura* (or, in China, the 'princelings' of the ruling party) resemble the political class we in the west already endure. Instead, his socialism would empower democratic decision-making in all the institutions in which socioeconomically significant issues are handled, starting with the workplace itself.

No democratic-socialist society has yet emerged, and Hägglund rejects a utopian blueprint for one. Political movements which promote such blueprints end up spawning unfree societies; the economic-liberal utopia of market society is the most important case in point. 'Democratic socialism' denotes a progressive developmental trend, not any sort of end state. Moreover, the forms of association in the pre-existing society, and the gradual process of transition itself, will leave their marks on what comes next. As will the vision and creativity of those who contribute to the transition.

During the ascendancy of welfare capitalism, which stagflation and the neoliberal ideological onslaught brought to an end in the late 1970s, many people saw it as having tamed capitalism and achieved goals antithetical to it: social security and social access for all, and a lessening of inequality, at least in life chances. The obvious weakness with this 'social democracy' was that it only ameliorated the capitalist mode of *distribution*, and left the mode of production itself unchanged. Its reforms were vulnerable to the economic-liberal counter-attack waiting in the wings.

In this sense, social democracy amounted to little more than social liberalism, based on the false premise that the mode of distribution can be separated from the mode of production. Like progressive thinkers going back to the founding of the socialist Second International in 1889, Hägglund values ameliorative reforms for their immediate improvement in the lot of the great majority. But as he shows, in themselves they don't initiate a transition to socialism, notwithstanding such claims in the programmes of the parties of labour that promoted these reforms.

The theorist and activist who masterminded the 1932

social-democratic breakthrough in Sweden, Ernst Wigforss, discerned and responded to this weakness, which repeatedly threatened to shrink his party's aspirations to mere social-liberal ones. In this way he grasped the challenge of transition. His legacy illustrates how we might approach transition today.[28]

In Sweden's democratic polity his party had to propose credible reforms to address immediate problems, starting with high unemployment and social distress during the Depression, in order to garner mass support and win majority government. But to the greatest possible extent, those reforms should be irreversible and seed new institutions that contribute to social transformation, Wigforss argued. To crystallise immediate goals, he advocated partial 'provisional utopias' to be successively replaced once achieved. His first provisional utopia, announced during the Depression, was full employment and social security. Once that was being achieved, he set up a new one – meaningful working lives and continuing choice of occupation, to be achieved through a labour-market board and industrial democracy.

When those reforms, too, found their way into the pipeline, he proposed the socialisation of the capital market to turn existing large corporations into 'social corporations without owners'. Existing shareholders would not be expropriated – their equity holdings would simply be turned into debenture stock without voting rights. The corporations would be answerable to society, and in the first instance to organised labour. This shift would radically change their forms of calculation and investment decisions.

When Wigforss retired from the social-democratic party's senior ranks in 1949, it began a slow retreat back to social liberalism. But the blue-collar peak union body, LO, stuck to Wigforss's conception. He had long nurtured a close association with this powerful body which already boasted the world's highest level of unionisation even before the social democrats came to power, but the successes of the social-democratic government from the 1930s nurtured LO's political creativity, making it an exemplar of an effective element in civil society. It deployed the labour-market board to offer workers a chance to change careers via well-funded retraining schemes that undercut their resistance when the industries that employed them had to be restructured. It mobilised around democratic reforms in enterprises and workplaces. And finally in 1976 it came up with a proposal to set up 'wage-earner funds', to socialise capital formation in large industrial corporations.

The proposal addressed the immediate problems of economic instability and insufficient industrial investment in the mid-1970s. Instead of being distributed as dividends, excessive profits would be ploughed back as working capital into the firms concerned, which would issue shares to their value to funds that the workforce controlled. Over a few years, these funds would have accumulated a controlling share in the firms involved, thus achieving economic democracy and economic citizenship for employees.[29] No existing private shareholders would be expropriated, but their voting power in general meetings would gradually be swamped.

Tragically, the social-democratic party reneged on its support for the proposal in the face of histrionic resistance from the right-wing parties and the employers' federation. So the proposal was defeated, and the party soon converted to neoliberalism, joining the many formerly reformist parties of labour in the western world in that camp. It too supported the shrinking and piecemeal privatisation of the welfare state, and lost ground electorally.

In spite of this dispiriting sequel, the Swedish case indicates how a democratic-socialist progression might work elsewhere on the basis of existing local institutional frameworks. It indicates what elements of a mobilised civil society, ones with clear ethical positions and a democratic-socialist vision, might have achieved in the face of corporate opposition if the state could be led to co-operate, or at least be neutralised.

Crouch's optimism about civil society's development seems justified. While I've been penning this chapter, it has sprung three pleasant surprises on me, on home soil. Firstly, the National Farmers' Federation (the peak council for Australian rural producers) has defied its affiliated National party by adopting a policy platform that sets a goal of net-zero carbon emissions by 2050.[30] The Nationals – along with the sitting conservative government of which they're a part – are members of 'the Carbon Club' and have steadfastly rejected that policy, but now stand to lose much of their electoral base. Secondly, in the same week, the board of AMP – a major financial institution in Australia – has come under attack from disgruntled investors (including pension funds) for not taking a sexual-harassment complaint seriously and for tolerating a misogynistic corporate culture. The chairman and one other director felt compelled to resign.[31] Thirdly, the global mining giant Rio Tinto has come under fire for blowing up an Aboriginal sacred site in the Juukan Gorge in Western Australia – two rock shelters containing evidence of continuous human use over 46,000 years, and of acknowledged archaeological significance – so as to extract the iron ore surrounding it. The company's grovelling public apology hasn't assuaged public and pension-fund investor opinion, or Indigenous resentment, The CEO and two other senior executives have been forced to resign.[32]

The latter two cases point to a promising shift in the balance of power from corporate to civic authority. One of neoliberalism's most prominent ideologues, Milton Friedman, taught that a company board's exclusive obligation is to maximise profit; it has no right (let alone obligation) to dabble in distractions like environmental protection, gender equality, and human and indigenous rights.[33] Yet here are paragons of neoliberal virtue being hung out to dry by civic mobilisation on ethical grounds, just for doing their job. It augurs well for a democratic-socialist transition driven by civil society.

The conflict between pension funds representing employees' social interests and the neoliberal government is now coming to a head, as the former have begun divesting their holdings in large corporations which ignore social demands, above all for a responsible climate policy. In a letter to the 200 largest companies listed on the Australian stock exchange, Debby Blakey, chief executive of one of the country's biggest superannuation funds, has required them to adopt the net-zero-by-2050 target and ensure women occupy at least forty per cent of their top positions. The government rebuked her in line with the Friedman doctrine: the funds' boards have just one legitimate function – profit maximisation – and she should stay in her lane. But she was not for turning. 'As a large asset owner, we obviously see engagement and exercising our vote as critically important in terms of being responsible investors,' she retorted. 'We want to be very clear with companies we invest in on our focus.'[34]

We can compare this conflict with the wage-earner fund proposal in Sweden mentioned above. Elements of civil society are becoming formidable players in financial markets (neoliberalism's holy of holies), bringing antithetical values and forms of calculation with them.

Let's end this chapter with a thought experiment. What would our lives look like in, say, thirty years' time, in a western society undergoing a transition to democratic socialism? We're still trucking, bartering and trading as Adam Smith would have us do – but now with more care and joy.

The changes are more obvious in the cities and towns. As we walk down the main street, we notice that the once-shuttered small shops have come back to life, as local businesses and creatives win back market shares from chain stores and global outfitters. (Most of yesteryear's gargantuan shopping malls have been repurposed as public recreational, meeting and performance spaces.) So street fashion exhibits more flair and variation. We're buying a lot more of our fresh produce from local famers' markets. The electric cars slipping past us emit neither noise nor exhaust fumes. But there aren't many of them; with a high-functioning public-transport system at hand, few of us can be bothered with the trouble and expense of owning a car. On the odd occasion we need one, we choose between the offerings of several car-share cooperatives.

Those who remember the bad old days might notice the absence of beggars and rough sleepers on the street, courtesy of restored social security and inclusiveness, and abundant invest-ment in social housing. They might also notice that the air is much cleaner and fresher; the burning of fossil fuels is approaching zero.

Even greater differences await us in our working lives. Some of us are self-employed or work in small businesses, but most of us work in large enterprises that take advantage of la-bour-saving technologies and scale economies – enterprises that we collectively own and control. Each work team figures out the best way to organise its own section. Some of us live and work in communities that once depended on extracting fossil fuels. But before those industries closed down the labour-market board en-couraged renewable-energy enterprises to begin operations in our communities, and it set up retraining institutes to prepare us to work in them. So most of us stayed in our communities, upskilled, and now work in the new industries. Some others decided to move to the city. None of us misses the grime, diseases and dangers of mining coal and fracking for gas.

We spend a lot less time at work, and we can negotiate and schedule our working hours flexibly. As a society we're only producing what we need and want, including what we intend to trade in exchange for goods we can't produce as easily as other countries can. We're not working to enrich remote, unproductive profit- and rent-seekers, and none of the value we produce leaks into tax havens. Communally-owned banks and pension funds provide us with the external finance we need from time to time to recapitalise our enterprises, or to set up new ones.

We pay high and progressive income taxes, and they're spent on our social needs – for education, health, income support, aged and disability care, infrastructure, public broadcasting, the arts, libraries etc., and for the administration of these boons. Now that they're no longer privatised or artificially corporatised, we don't run these institutions as profit-seeking enterprises. Today they're organised to efficiently serve their actual functions of social provision, care and improvement. It's all part of a wider change: care now drives our social and institutional lives. Greed and fear borne of social insecurity have been dethroned.

Apart from contributing our taxes, we don't pay for private schools or private hospitals and health insurance, because we already have access to best-quality health and education free of charge. We've put paid to the private affluence/public squalor syndrome of neoliberal capitalism. The government allocates three percent of its budget to foreign aid, giving priority to schemes that help recipient countries to implement their own development strategies, ones that don't involve labour-repressive enterprises or open access to foreign goods that crowd out local producers.

The eclipse of corporate power with its attendant political corruption has also called time on the political class and its multi-medial manipulative humbug. Elections and election campaigns have once more become occasions for us citizens to thrash out our social priorities and work out the best answers to the contingencies that arise in public life, free of static. Since these democratic processes once more make a real difference, political participation has soared at national, regional and local levels.

Because we work less, we have more time and energy to pursue other aspirations and interests. We participate in political and civic movements as active citizens. We spend more time with our children, though they also enjoy free and well-resourced day-care centres and preschools even before they hit their school years. We have more time to paint, draw, write, read, meditate, discuss, and hang out with family and friends. And to take stimulating courses in universities and adult-education institutes, and to go on excursions into nature. Some of us choose to sign up for the many enriching residential retreats that are on offer.

The thing is, we're freer than humans have ever been, and have more choices to pursue than ever before. Yet we sense a return to some features that pre- and non-capitalist societies have also exhibited, above all social inclusion and security, and a natural world no longer under existential threat.

The Buddha once captured a sense of his awakening experience in a parable. While wandering through a forest, a man comes across an ancient path or road, one evidently travelled by people in the past. He follows this path, and it leads him to the ruins of an ancient city, an ancient capital, 'with parks, groves, ponds and ramparts, a delightful place'. He reports his find to the king or royal minister, and recommends that the city be renovated. The king or royal minister so orders, 'and some time later that city would become successful and prosperous, well populated, filled with people, attained to growth and expansion.'[35]

The imagery here tells us that the ancient city is well endowed with public amenities (palatial private homes aren't mentioned), and that the community that has resettled it is thriving. Nevertheless, the story goes on to suggest that the people are thriving because they're practising the dharma. Which must mean that they're ordinary people dealing skilfully with the usual vicissitudes of human life, starting with birth and death. This is no paradisal communion of saints preserved forever in nirvanic suspended animation. And the people are thriving because they've restored something valuable that was already there for them; they haven't started from scratch.

The parable grasps the important restorative aspect of the democratic-socialist project, which in the first instance works towards a final victory for Polanyi's 'self-protection of society' in its two-centuries-long struggle against economic-liberal destructiveness. The project involves restoring the normal attributes of human community – inclusiveness, social security, and economic activity calibrated to serve social values and priorities. Only now it's not just a question of protecting society, but also the biosphere itself, from the same capitalist threat. And the social values and priorities in question all proceed from an ethic of care and an aspiration to promote spiritual freedom.

Conclusion

Two and a half millennia ago there lived a man called Gotama in a recently prosperous part of India, though one in which warring grandees put life at risk. He confronted the inescapable vicissitudes we humans all face – birth, death, ageing, sickness, separation, unpleasant associations, frustration, and our psycho-physical frailty. He developed a practice to work with these difficulties in a creative way so that they ultimately fuelled full human flourishing. The practice rested on an ethic of care and an investigative approach to meditation. Gotama elaborated a matrix of concepts ('the dharma') that people could deploy to parse and transform their own life experiences and inner lives. In this way he drew a diverse following, attracted the title of Buddha, and founded the tradition of dharma practice.

It remains a living tradition to this day, and has never stood still. From the time of his death, his tradition morphed into an institutionalised religion (later retrofitted with the title 'Buddhism') with all that this implies. Metaphysical beliefs came to mask and skew the matrix of concepts; practice was ritualised and regimented; followers were divided along lines of gender, civil status (monastic/lay) and rank; and the religious hierarchs entered into symbiotic relationships with temporal powers. These factors blunted the dharma's effectiveness in opening up the inner life, such that it functioned mainly as a conservative basis for social cohesion and political legitimation.

The religious turn might well have deadened the living tradition but for a sprinkling of dissenters in each generation, and the dharma's own spread to other cultures and societies. Each such entry became the occasion for a fresh look at the original dharma as a prelude to the creative work of reissuing it in the new language, set of cultural reference points, and historical circumstances. The dharma reanimated especially vigorously when it entered new host cultures in which institutional religion played a smaller role in bolstering temporal power in the guise of a national religion.

In our own time dharma practice has spread to every inhabited continent on earth, including western countries in which the authority of institutional religion had dwindled in recent times, leaving a hiatus in 'the western search for meaning'. Buddhism became one of the many contenders seeking to resolve this hiatus. It initially arrived in ancestral forms with immigrant Asian communities, then as a partially laicised 'Buddhist modernism' which made inroads into western societies from the 1960s. As a hybrid form, Buddhist modernism preserved too many elements of Asian ancestral religious schools to embed itself in late-modern western culture. Secular Buddhism began to crystallise during the first decade of this century in an effort to overcome that limitation.

'Secular' here refers principally to the temporal dimension – to the fact that we ourselves and everyone and everything that constitute our life-worlds begin, endure for a while, and then pass away, *in time*. Secularity eschews revelations and beliefs about entities and forms of existence outside of time.

Like the Buddha himself, it has no truck with metaphysical truth-claims. Secularity insists that thought and practice should address particular times and circumstances. Like their forerunners in other new host societies, secular Buddhists return to the original teachings for answers to some perennial questions – 'How should I live?' and 'What sort of person should I become?' – and new ones generated by the possibilities and dangers we're encountering now.

Like the Buddha himself, we in the west today are living through a period of great upheaval. We can cultivate the dharmic ethic of care by overthrowing long-established religious, social and political certitudes, oftentimes enjoying opportunities to challenge inured injustices such as patriarchy, racism and xenophobia. But we ourselves, our civilisation, and the very biosphere have now come under imminent existential threat from climate change.

To make the most of our dharma practice under these circumstances, we have to also dig deep in our own history and culture. By identifying the dharma's western affinities we can realise its potential to enrich our lives and to deepen into the human estate. In this way, too, we can situate ourselves in the history of our own societies, so developing an understanding of how our current dangers and opportunities have arisen, and how best to respond to them creatively in accordance with our ethic of care.

We now live in an interconnected world facing a catastrophe which we humans have conjured forth. We must break with the old idea that nice Buddhists steer clear of worldly affairs, especially politics; we must extend our ethical and spiritual practice precisely into these areas. Here we find the immediate drivers of climate change reside in a global capitalist system and the regressive policy regime of neoliberalism that is pushing us towards the brink.

At great cost to the social and the natural worlds, the current socio-economic system once performed a progressive role in spawning science and industry. But it has now outlived its ability to contribute to human well-being, and only its barbaric destructivity remains.

To honour their ethic of care, secular Buddhists can lend a hand in restoring environmental responsibility, social control over productive resources, and social cohesion and fairness. This project requires a gradual transition to a new socio-economic system – democratic socialism.

The processes that can build it are already on foot.

Notes

1   See Christian 2018, esp. chapter 11.
2   Numbers in brackets hereafter refer to the numbered paragraphs that constitute the encyclical.
3   Klein 2016.
4   See Wilkinson 2020.
5   Ghosh 2017: 89–90.
6   See Freeden 1978.
7   Quoted in Christian 2018: 296.
8   The best study of how institutions work that I know of is Tomlinson 2006.
9   See Browning 2017.
10   The grim pattern is laid out at length in Piketty 2014. To take just one of his teeming examples: in the USA in 2010, the richest one percent of the population owned 35 percent of capital wealth and banked 20 percent of national income – as against the bottom fifty percent's 5 and 20 percent respectively. On then-current trends, by 2030 the top one percent will receive 25 percent of total income, while the poorest half of the population will receive just 15 percent of national income (Tables 7.2 and 7.3). More recently, Thomas Piketty (2020) has examined the ideological mainsprings of today's ballooning inequalities.
11   See Crouch 2011.
12   Weber 2001: 124.
13   Lust, gluttony, greed, sloth, wrath, envy, pride.
14   Crouch 2011: ix.
15   Wilkinson 2020.
16   According to a statement released on 28.8.20 by the Australian Climate Roundtable – which includes peak business and industry bodies, as well as the peak union council: 'Australia is currently woefully unprepared for the scale of climate change threats that will emerge over the coming decades. There is no systemic government response (federal, state and local) to build resilience to climate risks. Action is piecemeal; uncoordinated; does not engage business, private sector investment, unions, workers in affected industries, community

sector and communities; and does not match the scale of the threat climate change represents to the Australian economy, environment and society' (*ACR* 2020). At the same time the Australian government unveiled a plan to divert public funds, earmarked for the development of clean energy, into encouraging private investment in the extraction of natural gas instead (*Sydney Morning Herald* 28.8.20). The fossil fuel in question has been enlisted as a 'transitional' source of energy in the mission to overcome a problem largely caused by fossil fuels. Marion Wilkinson (2020) uncovers the roots of this recalcitrance in her aptly titled book, *The Carbon Club*.

17 See Reinert 2007. According to the Global Slavery Index, there were 40.3 million slaves in the world in 2016, and the number is growing. Their products are regularly identified in the supply chains of major western retailers, especially in the clothing industry.

18 An outstanding early example is Pope Leo XIII's forceful encyclical, *Rerum novarum* of 1891 – a worthy predecessor to Francis's 2015 *Laudato Si'*.

19 Crouch 2015 provides an excellent account of precisely how privatisation degrades the social services in question.

20 Reinert 2007.

21 Klein 2016.

22 Crouch 2011.

23 See Higgins 2009.

24 Crouch 2015: 178.

25 Ehnmark 1986.

26 Hägglund 2020: 313.

27 Hägglund 2020: 376.

28 See Higgins & Dow 2013 for what follows.

29 A sympathetic critic of the plan, Walter Korpi (1983), pointed out that the funds would have been even more democratic if their board members were elected by the general electorate.

30 NFF 2020.

31 https://www.abc.net.au/news/2020-08-24/amp-chair-david-murray-director-john-fraser-resign-boe-pahari/12588366

32 'Rio top brass quit over role in caves blast', *Sydney Morning Herald*, 12.9.20.

33 Friedman 1970.

34 'HESTA calls for emission cuts, equality', *Sydney Morning Herald*, 24.9.20.

35 *Saṃyutta Nikāya* 12: 605.

References

ACR – Australian Climate Roundtable (2020) 'Far-reaching climate change risks to Australia must be reduced and managed' https://www.australianclimateroundtable.org.au/wp-content/uploads/2020/08/ACR_statement_on_climate_impacts-August_2020.pdf

Anālayo (2003), *Satipaṭṭhāna: the direct path to realization* (Birmingham: Windhorse)

Batchelor, Stephen (1983), *Alone with others: an existential approach to Buddhism* (New York: Grove Press)

_____ (1997), *Buddhism without beliefs: a contemporary guide to awakening* (New York: Riverhead)

_____ (2010), *Confession of a Buddhist atheist* (New York: Spiegel & Grau)

_____ (2012), 'A secular Buddhism', *Journal of Global Buddhism*, vol. 13, pp. 88–89

_____ (2015), *After Buddhism: rethinking the dharma for a secular age* (New Haven & London: Yale University Press)

_____ (2017), *Secular Buddhism: imagining the dharma in an uncertain world* (New Haven & London: Yale University Press)

_____ (2020), *The art of solitude: a meditation on being alone with others in this world* (New Haven & London: Yale University Press)

Batchelor, Martine and Stephen (2019), *What is this? Ancient questions for modern minds* (Wellington: Tuwhiri)

Bechert, Heinz (1966), *Buddhismus, Staat und Gesellschaft in den Ländern des Theravāda Buddhismus.* (3 vols; first vol: Berlin: Alfred Metzner)

Bellah, Robert (1970), *Beyond belief: essays on religion in a post-traditional world* (New York: Harper & Row)

Benhabib, Seyla (1992), *Situating the self: gender, community and postmodernism in contemporary ethics* (Cambridge: Polity)

Bollas, Christopher (2018), *Meaning and melancholia: life in the age of bewilderment* (Oxford: Routledge, 2018)

Browning, Christopher ([1992] 2017), *Ordinary men: Reserve Police Battalion 101 and the final solution in Poland* (New York: HarperPerennial)

Bubna-Litic, David, and Winton Higgins (2007), 'The rise of secular insight practice in Australia', *Journal of Global Buddhism* 8, pp. 157–173

Buddhaghosa, Bhadantācariya (1956), *The path of purification (Visuddhimagga).* Transl. Bhikkhu Ñānamoli. (Singapore: Singapore Buddhist Meditation Centre)

Burnouf, Eugène ([1844] 2010), *Introduction to the history of Indian Buddhism.* Transl. Katia Buffetrille & Donald S. Lopez Jr. (Chicago & London: University of Chicago Press)

Camus, Albert ([1947] 2001), *The plague* (Trans. Robin Buss. London and NY: Penguin)

Carrette, Jeremy, and Richard King (2005), *Selling spirituality: the silent takeover of religion* (London & New York: Routledge)

Christian, David (2018), *Origin story: a big history of everything* (London: Allen Lane)

Critchley, Simon (2001), *Continental philosophy: a very short introduction* (Oxford: Oxford University Press)

Crouch, Colin (2004), *Post-democracy* (Cambridge: Polity)

_____ (2011), *The strange non-death of neoliberalism* (Cambridge: Polity)

_____ (2015), *The knowledge corrupters: hidden consequences of the financial takeover of public life* (Cambridge: Polity)

Cupitt, Don (1997), *After God: the future of religion* (London: Weidenfeld & Nicolson)

Dawson, Geoff, and Liz Turnbull (2006), 'Is mindfulness the new opiate of the masses? Critical reflections from a Buddhist perspective', *Psychotherapy in Australia* vol.12 no.4, pp. 2–6

Didion, Joan (2007), *The year of magical thinking* (NY: Knopf)

_____ (2011), *Blue nights* (London: Fourth Estate)

Douglas, Mary ([1966] 1978), *Purity and danger: an analysis of concepts of pollution and taboo* (London, Boston & Henley: Routledge & Kegan Paul)

References

Eco, Umberto (2004), *The name of the rose* (London: Vintage)

Ehnmark, Anders (1986), *Maktens hemligheter: en essä om Machiavelli* ('The secrets of power: an essay on Machiavelli'. Stockholm: Norstedts)

Faure, Bernard (2009) *Unmasking Buddhism* (West Sussex: Wiley-Blackwell)

Flanagan, Owen (2011) *The bodhisattva's brain: Buddhism naturalized* (Camb. Mass.: MIT Press)

Foucault, Michel (1977), *Discipline and punish: the birth of the prison* (Trans. A. Sheridan. London: Penguin)

_____ (1980), *Power/knowledge: selected interviews and other writings 1972–1977* (Colin Gordon ed.; New York: Pantheon)

Francis, Pope (2015), *Laudato Si': on care for our common home* (San Francisco: St Ignatius Press)

Freeden, Michael (1978), *The new liberalism: an ideology of social reform* (Oxford: Clarendon)

Friedman, Milton (1970), 'The social responsibility of business is to increase its profits', *New York Times Magazine*, 13.9.70

Geering, Lloyd (1992), *Religious trailblazers.* (Wellington: St Andrew's Trust for the Study of Religion and Society)

_____ (2007), 'The Antipodean Christian', in Paul Morris and Mike Grimshaw (eds) *The Lloyd Geering reader* (Wellington: Victoria University Press)

Ghosh, Amitav (2017), *The great derangement: climate change and the unthinkable* (Chicago: University of Chicago Press)

Global Slavery Index (2018), *Global findings* (https://www.globalslaveryindex. org/2018/findings/global-findings accessed 27.8.20)

Gombrich, Richard and Gananath Obeyesekere (1988), *Buddhism transformed: religious change in Sri Lanka* (Princeton: Princeton University Press)

Greenfield, Susan (2008), *ID: the quest for identity in the 21st century* (London: Sceptre)

Grose, Peter (2014), *A good place to hide* (Sydney: Allen & Unwin)

Hägglund, Martin (2020), *This life: secular faith and spiritual freedom* (New York: Anchor Books)

Heidegger, Martin ([1927] 2008), *Being and time.* Transl. John Macqarrie and Edward Robinson. (New York & London: HarperPerennial)

Higgins, Winton (2009), 'Standardizing corporate social responsibility' in David Bubna-Litic (ed.) *Spirituality and corporate social responsibility: interpenetrating worlds* (Farnham, Surrey: Gower)

Higgins, Winton, and Geoff Dow (2013), *Politics against pessimism: social democratic possibilities since Ernst Wigforss* (Bern, CH: Peter Lang AG)

Horne, Donald ([1964] 2008), *The lucky country* (Melbourne: Penguin)

Inwood, Michael (1999), *A Heidegger dictionary* (Oxford: Blackwell)

James, William ([1902] 1994), *The varieties of religious experience* (New York:
    Modern Library)

Keynes, John Maynard (1936), *The general theory of employment, interest, and
    money* (London: Palgrave Macmillan)

Klein, Naomi (2016), 'Let them drown: the violence of othering in a warming
    world', *London Review of Books* v. 38 n. 11 (2.6.16)

Kornblatt, Joyce (2020), *Mother tongue* (Blackheath, NSW: Brandl & Schlesinger)

Korpi, Walter (1983), *Från undersåte till medborgare: om fonder och ekonomisk
    demokrati* ('From underling to citizen: on funds and economic democracy')
    (Stockholm: Tidens Debatt no. 3)

Kuzminski, Adrian (2008), *Pyrrhonism: how the ancient Greeks reinvented
    Buddhism* (Lanham: Lexington)

Laqueur, Thomas (2015), *The work of the dead: a cultural history of mortal remains*
    (Princeton: Princeton University Press)

Lasch, Christopher (1979), *The culture of narcissism: American life in an age of
    diminishing expectations* (New York: Norton)

Leader, Darian (2009), *The new black: mourning, melancholia and depression*
    (London: Penguin)

Ling, Trevor (1973), *The Buddha: Buddhist civilization in India and Ceylon*
    (Hammondsworth, Middlesex: Penguin)

Lopez, Donald S. Jr (2002), *A modern Buddhist bible: essential readings from east and
    west* (Boston: Beacon Press)

_____ (2008), *Buddhism & science: a guide for the perplexed* (Chicago and London:
    University of Chicago Press)

MacIntyre, Alasdair (1985), *After virtue* (2nd edn. London: Duckworth)

McMahan, David (2008), *The making of Buddhist modernism* (New York: Oxford
    University Press)

Magid, Barry (2008), *Ending the pursuit of happiness: a Zen guide* (Boston: Wisdom)

Malalasekera, GP ([1938] 1997), *Dictionary of Pāli proper names* (3 vols. Oxford:
    Pali Text Society)

MAPPG (Mindfulness All-Party Parliamentary Group) (2015), *Mindful nation UK:
    report by MAPPG* (London: Mindfulness Initiative)

Marshall, Thomas Humphrey (1950), *Citizenship and social class and other essays*
    (Cambridge: Cambridge University Press)

References

Mercier, Pascal (2008), *Night train to Lisbon* (Transl. Barbara Harshav. New York: Grove Press)

Merleau-Ponty, Maurice (1962), *Phenomenology of perception* (London: Routledge & Kegan Paul)

_____ (1968), *The visible and the invisible* (Evanstown: Northwestern University Press)

Mishra, Pankaj (2004), *An end to suffering: the Buddha in the world* (London: Picador)

Ñāṇamoli, Bhikkhu ([1972] 1992), *The life of the Buddha according to the Pali canon* (Seattle: BPS Parivatti Editions)

Ñāṇavīra Thera ([1965] 2001), *Clearing the path: writings of Ñāṇavīra Thera (1960–1965)*. Vol. 1 (Dehiwala, Sri Lanka: Buddhist Cultural Centre)

Nārada Maha Thera (1979), *A comprehensive manual of Abhidhamma*. 4th edition. (Kuala Lumpur: Buddhist Missionary Society)

NFF (National Farmers Federation) (2020), *Climate change policy* (Canberra: NFF)

Norman, KR ([1982] 2003), *Collected papers*. Vol. II (Oxford: Pali Text Society)

Nussbaum, Martha (1990), *Love's knowledge: essays in philosophy and literature* (New York & Oxford: Oxford University Press)

Phillips, Adam (2012), *Missing out: in praise of the unlived life* (Penguin: London)

Phillips, Adam, and Barbara Taylor (2009), *On kindness* (London: Hamish Hamilton)

Piketty, Thomas (2014), *Capital in the twenty-first century* (Transl. Arthur Goldhammer. Cambridge Mass. & London: Belknap/Harvard University Press)

_____ (2020), *Capital and ideology* (Transl. Arthur Goldhammer. Cambridge Mass. & London: Belknap/Harvard University Press)

Pocock, J. G. A. (2006), 'Present at the creation: with Laslett to the lost worlds', *International Journal of Public Affairs* 2, 7–17

Poole, Steven (2013), 'Life's more complicated than this', *Guardian Weekly*, 1 February 2013

Prochnik, George (2015), *The impossible exile: Stefan Zweig at the end of the world* (New York: Other Press)

Purser, Ronald E (2019), *McMindfulness: how mindfulness became the new capitalist spirituality* (London: Repeater)

Reinert, Erik (2007), *How rich countries got rich...and why poor countries stay poor* (London: Constable)

Rockhill, W. Woodville (transl.) (1884), *The life of the Buddha and the early history of his order: derived from Tibetan works in the Bkah-hgyur and Bstan-hgyur* (London: Trübner)

Rorty, Richard (2001), *Essays on Heidegger and others: philosophical papers* (New York: Cambridge University Press)

Rose Hilary, and Steven Rose (2012), *Genes, cells and brains: bioscience's Promethean claims* (London: Verso)

Safran, Jeremy (ed.) (2003), *Psychoanalysis and Buddhism: an unfolding dialogue* (Boston: Wisdom)

Siff, Jason (2010), *Unlearning meditation: what to do when instructions get in the way* (Boston & London: Shambhala)

Smee, Sebastian (2018), *Net loss: the inner life in the digital age* (Melbourne: Quarterly Essay no. 72)

Smith, Ronald Gregor (1966), *Secular Christianity* (New York: Harper & Row)

Strachey, James, and Anna Freud (transl. and eds) (1957), *The standard edition of the complete psychological works of Sigmund Freud* (London: the Hogarth Press), vol. 14

Tambiah, Stanley Jayaraja (1992), *Buddhism betrayed: religion, politics, and violence in Sri Lanka* (Chicago: University of Chicago Press)

Taylor, Barbara (2014), *The last asylum: a memoir of madness in our times* (London & NY: Hamish Hamilton)

Taylor, Charles (1989), *Sources of the self: the making of the modern identity* (Cambridge: Cambridge University Press)

_____ (2006), 'Engaged agency and background in Heidegger', in Charles Guignon (ed.) *The Cambridge companion to Heidegger.* 2nd edition (Cambridge & New York: Cambridge University Press)

_____ (2007), *A secular age* (Cambridge Mass. & London: Belknap)

Tomlinson, Jim ([1981] 2006), *Problems in British economic policy 1870–1945* (Oxford: Routledge)

Twenge, Jean, and Keith Campbell (2009), *The narcissism epidemic: living in the age of entitlement* (New York: Free Press)

Vattimo, Gianni (2002), *After Christianity* (Transl. Luca d'Isanto. New York & Chichester: Columbia University Press)

_____ (2011), *A farewell to truth* (Trans. William McCuaig. New York: Columbia University Press)

Victoria, Brian (2006), *Zen at war* (2nd edition. Lanham: Rowman & Littlefield)

Voyce, Malcolm (2017), *Foucault, Buddhism and disciplinary rules* (Oxford:

References

Routledge)

Wallace, B Alan (2010), 'Distorted visions of Buddhism: agnostic and atheist',
    Mandala Publications (http://mandalamagazine.org/archives/mandala-
    issues-for-2010/october)

Watson, Peter (2014), *The age of atheists: how we have sought to live since the death of
    God* (New York: Simon & Schuster)

Weber, Max ([1905] 2001), *The Protestant ethic and the spirit of capitalism* (Transl.
    Talcott Parsons. London: Routledge)

Wilkinson, Marian (2020), *The Carbon Club* (Sydney: Allen & Unwin)

Woodhead, Linda, and Paul Heelas (2000), *Religion in modern times: an
    interpretive anthology* (Oxford and Malden, Mass.: Blackwell)

Woodward, FL, transl. ([1930] 1993), *The book of kindred sayings (Samyutta nikāya).*
    Part IV (Oxford: Pali Text Society)

Canonical sources

Aṅguttara nikāya (The numerical discourses of the Buddha). (Transl. Bhikkhu
    Bhodi. Somerville MA: Wisdom Publications, 2012)

Majjhima nikāya (The middle length discourses of the Buddha). (Trans. Bhikkhus
    Ñāṇamoli and Bodhi, 2nd edn. Somerville MA: Wisdom Publications, 2001)

Saṃyutta nikāya (The connected discourses of the Buddha). Transl. Bhikkhu Bhodi.
    Somerville MA: Wisdom Publications, 2000)

Thanks

I want to thank Ramsey Margolis for suggesting that I prepare a manuscript containing a selection of essays and talks on secular Buddhism, and (as The Tuwhiri Project's major contributor) seeing the manuscript through all its stages to publication.

I would also like to thank my practice community, Kookaburra Sangha, for its friendship and dynamism, and for giving me feedback on some of the ideas contained in this book. In the same vein I thank other lay sanghas who have invited me to speak and made helpful comments: One Mindful Breath in Wellington, Aotearoa New Zealand, and Bluegum, Golden Wattle and Northern Beaches sanghas in and around Sydney.

I thank the School of International Studies and Education in the Faculty of Arts and Social Sciences at the University of Technology Sydney for providing me with collegiality, space and resources as I produced this text.

I'm also grateful to John Houston, our London designer, for his good work, not least in adorning the text with examples of the Australian fauna I grew up with. Sadly, climate change and profligate land clearance now threaten two of these species – the koala and the platypus – with extinction.

Last but not least, I thank my partner Lena, our daughters Freya and Torunn, and our grandchildren Indra, Ronja and Lotta, for their love, support and forbearance as I wrote and edited the pieces collected in this volume. They also kept my feet on the ground (and occasionally to the fire) – an essential service to a writer otherwise in thrall to his keyboard.

FINDING MEANING IN A DIFFICULT WORLD

The Tuwhiri Project is the initiative of secular dharma practitioners in Australia and Aotearoa New Zealand. A word in te reo Maori, 'tuwhiri' means to disclose, to reveal, to divulge, to make known, or a clue, a means of discovering or disclosing something lost or hidden, a hint, a tip, a pointer.

The secular approach to the dharma is a trend in contemporary western Buddhism which highlights the fundamental ethic of the teachings of Gotama, the historical Buddha – care – in all its aspects. Secularity calls on us to express this ethic of care in ways appropriate to our time and current predicaments.

Our intention is to produce educational resources for secular dharma practitioners and communities. The Tuwhiri Project is 100 percent owned by Aotearoa Buddhist Education Trust (ABET), a New Zealand registered charity. As a social enterprise with no investor shareholders and so no need to prioritise profit-making, we can focus on our purpose: to help people find meaning in a difficult world.

To find out how you can support The Tuwhiri Project, please go to:

https://www.tuwhiri.nz/about

CPSIA information can be obtained
at www.ICGtesting.com
Printed in the USA
BVHW061543231121
622343BV00011B/328